Idiots in Iceland

A Guide, Companion and Resource

EINBREIÐ BRÚ

Hróðbjartur Ísarngarðar Kyndilsson

Idiots In Iceland
Version 1
©Hróðbjartur Ísarngarðar Kyndilsson 2017
ISBN 978-9935-24-099-6

Topics

1. Idiots' Destination

Congratulations! You've bought a tourist guide book with an edge. These pages are written for, by, and about, idiots. They will not tell you what you want to hear, but rather what you need to know (yes all right, and some things you neither want nor need to hear or know). In any case, this is the kind of information you just don't get elsewhere - probably. If reading these pages saves your life, as it well could, you are up on the whole deal. It's very likely you will also get your money back and then some if you follow its advice.

The aim of this work is fourfold:

1. To enlighten
2. To entertain
3. To save your life
4. To save Iceland from you

Why do people come to Iceland? For a long time they didn't, because they couldn't. Then they could, but still didn't. It was cold, boring, badly located and seriously uncool. The few people who did visit were mostly German weirdos, and they are the worst kind of weirdos. Then, surprisingly, it became cool. For this transformation there were four main reasons:

1. Bjork
2. Bjørk
3. Björk
4. It got warmer

Which spelling is correct? Wrong! In 1993 Björk burst upon the world music scene like an atomic powered Spanish Slug (btw. the Germans have nothing on Björk). She made some big name acquaintances in London who realized Iceland's potential cool factor, came to Reykjavík for partying, and what do you know, Iceland had achieved coolness almost overnight. At around the same time, the climate started to improve gradually so a visit to Iceland became less a protracted torture session and more an interesting discomfort. It seems a thing can become warm and cool at the same time, but I digress. The ball started rolling with Björk, and a quarter of a century later, here we are - tourist hell.

There is no getting around it, Iceland does indeed contain a stupendously large number of terribly interesting natural, mostly geological, features. Also, Icelandic culture is unique and amazing, yaddi-yadda. Which one of the following is true?

1. Let's not go to Iceland, it's a silly place[1]

2. Each average size family in Iceland can claim one square km and 250 geological features

3. You will not be murdered here

4. The locals like you

5. You can pay a lot of money to swim in industrial waste

6. All of the above

Wrong again! It's actually 6. A tourist was brutally murdered by a local nutcase in 1982. That has not recurred to best knowledge, so statistically you're golden. It's pretty safe for the locals too. The clearance rate for murder cases is 100% going back almost 50 years. Being blown up, machinegunned, or machete'd, which is now a near-certainty if you visit Syria (or Paris), will not happen to you while in Iceland. Probably.

The locals are still mostly positive toward you. Mostly. That could change.

Iceland is silly. Icelanders generally are members of the International Movement of Scandinaivism, well known for the gullibility of its members. For example, in 19th century North America, scandi immigrants got a reputation for being stupid. This reputation was most likely earned through being fooled and cheated by all the other ethnic groups. The scandis mostly solved this problem by sticking to their own. Also, they eventually got wise. Just ask the James-Younger gang. Reading these pages, you may get the impression that I am sort of a jerk, and that most Icelanders then are the

---

[1]From "Monty Python and the Holy Glacier"

same. Alas, this is not so (the latter part). They are mostly idiots of the children's-play, everybody-is-my-friend variety. The normal Icelander is plagued by Scandinaivism, and in particular the branch of that movement known as Egnerism. Thorbjörn Egner, a Norwegian author of children's plays, has corrupted more minds than Sun Myung Moon, John Travolta and Charles Manson put together. Icelanders watch these plays as children, and then they watch them again as adults with their own children. Curiously, they start to believe the message contained in them, that every threat and enemy can be neutralized with soft-spoken words. The cause is not helped by the fact that Icelanders have never been in the position to carry the responisbility for their own national security. With a spot of goodwill, the national motto can be presented as stolen from the Beatles: "You know it's gonna be all right". It is amazing how often it has actually worked out that way.

Point 5.... it's technically true. I'm not going to explain. If you bump into me hiking out there, you can ask me.

Point 2? Geography. Do your own math.

Welcome to *Mordor*

Unhelpful Destinations

This is not your regular kind of travel brochure. Not a lot of space will be devoted to destinations and attractions, such information is widely available elsewhere and is not a main purpose of this book. A few notes will be made, with emphasis on thinking outside the box (hateful phrase - sorry), ideas and information you might not find elsewhere. Some maps will be provided; these may seem of poor quality (OK, they are). The features highlighted are mostly those mentioned in this and later chapters, for clarity. Use these as a reference. A tourist of your calibre, who has equipped him/herself with a Guidebook with a Difference, surely possesses a proper map. Use that for navigation. I went so far as to throw in bits of local history. If you want to find out more, *wikipedia* is your friend. If you don't, I apologize in advance. These don't go up to 11.

1. Reykjavík

The only proper city in Iceland, and a beautiful one at that. In terms of the human body, it is almost as beautiful as an impacted toenail in the process of dropping off. In terms of The War of the Worlds, and the Martians have landed, Reykjavík city centre is ground zero. It is absolutely crawling with tourists for most if not all of the year.

Reykjavík was the first historical homestead (see chapter 2). Then for a long time nothing happened, with very few mentions in sagas or annals. At the end of the 18th century the first capital investment company was formed, in the tiny village of Reykjavík. The company failed, but Reykjavík continued to develop as a center of trade and administration. Today it is a Metropolitan Centre of culture and wisdom, complete with Penis Museum. Events defining Reykjavík as a capital city begin only as late as the 19th century. The town mostly expanded in the 20th century. This is why when two Reykjavíkians meet they ask each other: *Where are you from?* That doesn't mean which side of Reykjavík, it means which part of Iceland.[2] It's a mushroom town, as if you couldn't tell? Old Reykjavík is the area west of *Snorrabraut* road, east of which was real countryside with pasture within living memory. The main shopping street downtown, *Laugavegur*, is so named because as a well-travelled footpath it led to *Laugardalur*, a site of hot springs (*"Laugar"*) and therefore a choice spot for doing laundry by the womenfolk of Reykjavík - perhaps worthy of a pilgrimage in the name of women's causes. The steam

---

[2] This author, for example, has three grandparents born in Reykjavík. That is an unusually high number for the generation who... went all weepy at the cinema when the circle closed on *Darth Vader*.

columns rising from this place gave the area its name originally - "*Reykjavík*" literally means *"Smokey Bay"*. Apart from the national church, by far the oldest Icelandic institution with continuous provenance is *Menntaskólinn í Reykjavík*, a secondary school. Founded as a church school at *Skálholt* in the late 11th century, it has been through several names and locations before ending up in Reykjavík city centre (large 19th c. building). Today, *"MR"* commands respect and jealousy in equal measure. How old is your high school?

The Reykjavík metropolitan area encompasses several municipalities and is home to two-thirds of the country's population. Outside Reykjavík proper, travelling south you have, in succession, *Kópavogur*, *Garðabær* and *Hafnarfjörður*.[3] These towns have a bit of history. Kópavogur was the spot where, in 1662, Icelanders signed up to Absolute Monarchy (a popular political brand of the era). Soldiers were on hand to rough up anybody reluctant to sign. *Hafnarfjörður* was an important natural harbor, frequented by rowdy English merchants and fishermen from the 15th century onwards. They were outfought and outcompeted by the Hamburg Hanse merchants, who traded there until ousted by Royal Monopoly. A peninsula to the south called *Álftanes* supports *Bessastaðir* homestead. This was the first Royal possession property in Iceland and through the centuries served as the seat of the Governor. Today it is the Presidential residence, clearly visible from Reykjavík's south shore.

Off the north shore of Reykjavík there's a dog-shaped island called *Viðey* (lit. Wood-Island, although today it sports no trees). It's a dreary place very nearly devoid of attractions, one of the many things you can waste your time on in Reykjavík. Not recommended.

Unless you're going to Keflavík Airport you leave Reykjavík heading east. The main road splits into the south leg of Route 1 which takes you to the southland, and the north leg of Route 1 which takes you

---

[3] The latter is the town of elves, apparently. That's ironic, because this characterization implies *idiots*. I thought you should know.

through *Mosfellsbær* to the westland. Note this location if you are driving yourself; the south route splits off to the right just before passing under the third overhead road bridge on the main route to the east. After Mosfellsbær, there's a second split between the westland and *Þingvellir*/southland.

Although I'm not a tourist, I have a strong feeling that Reykjavík is a boring city to discover. I suppose you are going to explore the city centre and I'm not going to try and stop you. After you've done that, there are some overlooked and interesting sites at least worth thinking about. One is *Öskjuhlíð*, specifically the south face below *Perlan*, the bowl-shaped restaurant on top of the water tanks. There, in the woods, you can pretend to forget you are in a city. Also it contains relics of the 1940 British occupation, including bunkers, pillboxes and artillery/ammunition pits. The hill overlooks Reykjavík Airport, which was originally built by the British army.

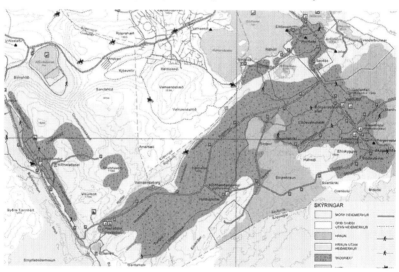

Map showing Heiðmörk and Lake Elliðavatn (top)

Another perhaps worthwhile stop is *Elliðaárdalur*, the river valley on the East Side. If you want a really long and interesting hike with-

10

out investing dearly in transportation, you can go to *Heiðmörk*, a park immediately east of inhabited Reykjavík. There you can really lose yourself, yet follow an extensive network of well-marked and mapped (and underused) paths. Recommended. Just stay away from *Breiðholt*, a semi-dangerous, east side ghetto.

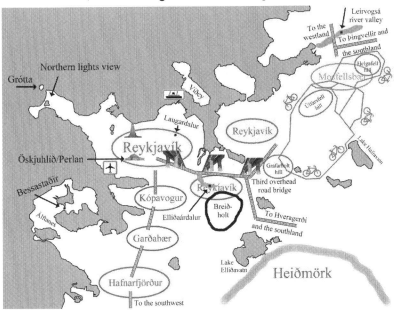

Reykjavík Metropolitan Area

Another option is to go cycling just north of *Heiðmörk*: *Grafarholt - Hafravatn - Mosfellbær - Grafarholt*. It's a circuit around the hill called *Úlfarsfell*. An optional extra circuit is around *Helgafell*, to the northeast (just close the gate behind you). You can utilize horse riding paths in the area, but be warned - if you notice anyone on horseback, dismount immediately, move off the path and wait for them to pass. Horses don't like bicycles, they could be spooked. Be further warned, this area is a bit rough and you'll have to figure out the paths a bit. Hint: Go wide.

Just north of *Helgafell* you find a river, *Leirvogsá*, worth exploring

11

for an hour or so. Nice element to a hiking/cycling tour. Also reachable by car, but beware those terrible roads! (See chapter 5).

All of the above destinations are reachable by local bus, or very nearly. So rent a bike and/or take the bus, and have a groovy time on a shoestring. Bring a packed lunch of local delicacies, and maybe something to drink (but mind laws on alcohol, see below).

• Music suggestion for driving ugly streets: Beastie Boys - *Sabotage*

2. Extreme Southwest (Reykjanes)

This is your most likely entry point into the country (*Keflavík* Airport). The major town in the area, located to the east of the airport, is officially named *Reykjanesbær*. The locals mostly use the older names of villages that make up the modern town. The north part is *Keflavík* and the south and east neighborhoods are *Njarðvík*. This could get confusing. There are further towns and villages, most notably *Grindavík* on the south coast, next to the *Blue Lagoon*. The history of the area is mostly that of fishing. You wouldn't believe it today, but near the "toe" of the peninsula there used to be a major agricultural homestead, *Kirkjuból*. The site is on the verge of disappearing into the fangs of the sea, but used to be centrally located on a sizable estate. It was the scene of brutal and pivotal events in the case of the "Bishop in a Bag". Some decades later it was again the scene of brutal, but this time ineffectual, events to do with the Reformation. See below and chapter 2 for details. An enormous influence on the local culture was the American air base, in operation since 1943. Keflavík especially was known for being ahead of the rest in terms of popular music and pop culture, but also for a lot of original musical talent to whom is dedicated an entire Rock Museum. This area has lots of geothermal activity, hot springs, pristine lava and moss. Interesting moderate climb with a great view is Mt. *Þorbjörn*, between *Grindavík* and the *Blue Lagoon*. Lake *Kleifarvatn* is striking, if not warm and welcoming. The *Krýsuvík* area is well worth a stop if you're cruising, and then don't forget the cliffs area down by the sea for some unique geological formations. Worthwhile to look at since there is no reason to hurry to get to Reykjavík, and why not chalk this bit off before heading inland? Do you want to visit the beach where Clint Eastwood filmed *Flag of Our Fathers*? It's there to the far west, *Stóra-Sandvík*. Don't bother with that 'Bridge between continents' crap though. If you want a tiny golden circle of your own, it's *Keflavík - Garður - Sandgerði - Hafnir - Njarðvík/Keflavík*. The road south from *Sandgerði* is a particularly charming one. Go by car (slow down for birds) or, on a fine day, bicycle (speed up to get away from birds). Note that this is a highway route. Take every precaution if cycling on the highway.

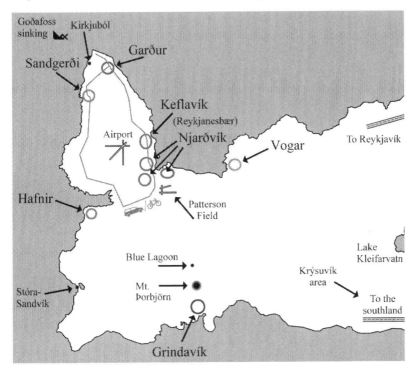

The Southwest/Reykjanes

• Music sugg. when exiting the Airport: Led Zeppelin - *Immigrant Song*

13

3. The Southland

The only area in Iceland that is flat, and feasible to navigate in two dimensions. That makes us locals a little bit confused, but you'll be OK. Mostly agriculture, and a few trees. The southland is the earthquake capital of Iceland, the traditional *Southland Quake* of magnitude up to 7 has wrought havoc over the centuries and tends to increase the output of hot springs but no longer threatens modern construction. This area is the agricultural powerhouse of Iceland, and historically very important. *Skálholt* is the original seat of the South Bishopric, effective capital of Iceland for 7 centuries or more, a town of more than a hundred people and a centre of learning.[4] Today, *Skálholt* is a ceremonial and historical exhibit. But what if you are a naughty Bishop? There is one example in *Jón Gerreksson*, a Danish questionable cleric who obtained the seat by bribing the pope. He arrived in 1426 with a retinue of "Lads", who proved to be troublemakers, unpopular with the locals. The Bishop himself went out of his way to humiliate locals of high stature. Things came to a head when the leader of the Lads (alleged Bish's bastard son) asked lady *Margrét* for her hand in marriage and was refused. In retaliation the spurned groom-to-be led an assault on her brother's estate at *Kirkjuból* where Margrét was staying. The homestead was burned to the ground and everyone on the estate was killed, except Margrét who dug her way out of the burning building and fled on horseback, declaring she would marry the guy who avenged her cause. There was no shortage of suitors. Armies of locals converged on *Skálholt*, dragged the Bishop down the aisle, put him in a bag and drowned him in the nearest river. The Lads were hunted down and killed to a man. Margrét married one of the leaders of this enterprise and they became the wealthiest couple in the land. How much more romantic can you get? - is what Quentin Tarantino is thinking.

---

[4]The northerners insisted they had to have a Bishop of their own, and eventually got their way. That's always the way with them, be it a Bishopric, a university, or a tunnel.

Another early centre of learning in Iceland was *Oddi*, the homestead of a powerful family that included *Sæmundur the Learned*, and later the home of a young *Snorri Sturluson* (see chapters 2 and 3). The most celebrated of all the sagas, *Njáls saga*, takes place in the southland (*Bergþórshvoll*). To the west you find *Þingvellir*, lots of history and nature going on there. This is where things happened in olden days, laws were made, deals were struck, judgements handed down - and not always peacefully. It may be interesting to some, that no serious archaeological dig has ever been undertaken in *Þingvellir*,

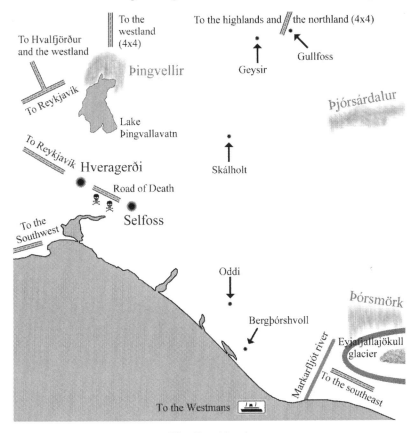

The Southland

although the fields there are expected to hold humongous treasure in those terms. When you've seen the main attractions on the west side of the valley, take a look at the woods area on the east side. It has paths, aboriginal type Birchwood forest and also planted evergreen forest, and a really cool rift canyon and great all round view. Farther east, *Geysir* (*"Gusher"*) is the original erupting hot spring, the Daddy spring. All other Geysers are named for him. Then there's *Gullfoss*, the best waterfall in the world. Don't fall in. More on that later. The northeast portion (i.e. upriver) of the southland has some pretty interesting, even mesmerizing waterways, well worth exploring. Why not pretend you're *Huckleberry Finn* and raft down to the coast? Just remember to step off in time. The Atlantic is not your friend (see chapter 5). Also, mind rapids and waterfalls. Well upriver to the east is *Þjórsárdalur*, including historical exhibit of a viking homestead (*Stöng*). *Þórsmörk* is a traditional haunt of Icelanders in summer for camping, drinking, singing and vomiting. You can't get there by normal car though, unbridged, everchanging glacial rivers. Rent a 4x4 (read chapter 5 first) or book a bus ride; bring a tent. Roughly speaking, the area east of *Þingvellir*, west of *Þjórsárdalur* and north of the ringroad holds a treasure of natural beauty and unusually still and clement weather. A lot of fun to explore by car or bicycle. Towns in the area include *Hveragerði* which is rather cool with interesting surroundings, and *Selfoss*, which is really dull. If your electric car runs out of juice in *Selfoss*, it's a fate worse than death. Warning: The bit of highway that runs between *Hveragerði* and *Selfoss* is the Road of Death - Iceland's worst accident blackspot, a high-speed road with bends and hills that obscure the driver's view. Never overtake on this road, even where legal.

• Music suggestion; car window rolled down: Lynyrd Skynyrd - *Sweet Home Alabama*

4. The Southeast

This area stretches roughly (west to east) from the river *Markarfljót* to the town of *Höfn*. It has a lot of ice. As if Europe's biggest glacier isn't enough, it has a couple more, and the *Ice Lagoon* too. It's a lagoon, but with ice (*Jökulsárlón*). It is incredibly conveniently located on the highway. It is a star of no less than five international blockbuster films. *Skaftafell* national park is wedged up there to the glacier with campsite, natural attractions and whatnot.

To the tourist, this is the roughest area of Iceland. General description: A strip of land wedged between hostile glaciers and an even more hostile Atlantic, regularly ripped apart by glacio-volcanic floods. If that's not hostile enough for you, it was also the site of the worst ever volcanic eruption in world history in terms of lives lost (*Laki*, 1783), and also the most annoying eruption ever in terms of travel and pronounciation (*Eyjafjallajökull*, 2010). Besides that, the best known historical event from this area is the *Sermon of Fire*; this is something for you religious types. On the 43rd day of the Laki eruption the lava flow had reached nearly within a mile of the

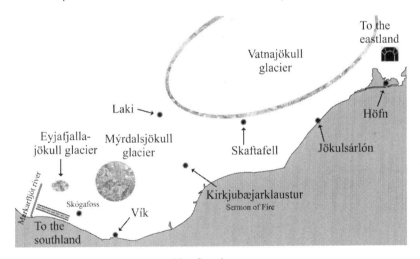

The Southeast

church at *Síða*. *Jón Steingrímsson*, since known as the *Fire Preacher*, held epic sermon to a packed congregation during which the lava

17

flow stopped, obviously through the power of prayer. But give the King some credit; when he heard what was happening to his most weird and vulnerable subjects he sent a big box of money to *Jón* for distribution among the farmers - just like the King of England did during the Potato Famine - right?

If you are passing by on the ringroad, do not fail to stop at *Skógafoss* waterfall. I have a dare for you there: Walk (or preferably run) all the way to the sandy rim of the lagoon below the waterfall and touch the water (and then go back). If you can, you are Worthy, and on the fast track to *Tourist of the Month*. If you want an inviting stopover, a sort of Rivendell experience, your best bet is *Kirkjubæjarklaustur* (short: *"Klaustur"*) (actually the only convenient stop between *Vík* and the eastfjords). It is magical, and it has elves if you choose to believe so. Wraiths roam the lava fields to the south, but you're safe inside the town. Many short hikes are available, and longer ones too. If you're a rugged outdoorsperson, you'll find many worthy challenges in the southeast.

• Music suggestion at the Ice Lagoon: Vanilla Ice - *Ice Ice Baby*

5. The Eastland

This area is sparsely populated and always has been. Therefore, even less has happened here than in other parts of Iceland so there are few historical details to bore you with. On the other hand, it's really pretty, and varied. If you approach from the south (or are leaving that way), mind that the road through *Öxi* pass is only open during summer, and is the kind of road that will cure your interest in rollercoasters. By the seaside you have your traditional fjords (*Eastfjords*) and fishing villages, but inland you find the *Shire* - the area around *Egilsstaðir* - unusually, a town only as old as *Las Vegas*.[5] A

---

[5] My plan for this area is for gambling to be legalized in this county exclusively. Egilsstaðir has an international airport so high rollers could jet in, shoot some reindeer, and throw them bones and flip them cards in the evening. It WOULD be Las Vegas. Nobody listens to me.

hugely untypical river/lake with its own serpent monster and also untypically, enough trees that if you are a tree-hugger you could get hugged out here (I did). Visit the forestry station and the surrounding woods on the south bank. If you travel west from there you can visit the highly contentious *Kárahnúkar* dam and don't forget to make a stop at *Skriðuklaustur* at the top of the lake. It has a really interesting, ongoing archaeological dig, unearthing for example alleged cases of pre-columbine syphilis - if you're interested in that sort of thing. The international ferry terminal is across the mountains on the far east coast at *Seyðisfjörður*. This was an important Allied base and port during WW2, and target of several air raids by the Germans. Going north from *Egilsstaðir* you will encounter quite accessible moon landscape with ridiculous hills and mountains, right there by the highway. You can also go off the beaten track for more of the same. On the main highway you find *Mývatn*, a popular attraction (Do me a favor and hold it in at *Mývatn*, it's a major battlefield of the Poop Wars, see chapter 4). Well to the northeast there's *Dettifoss* waterfall (star of *Prometheus*), and *Ásbyrgi* (*Sleipnir*'s hoofprint). A lot of bang for your buck, and very few locals to get in your way and/or annoy. Recommended.

The Eastland

• Music suggestion while riding along the river-lake *Lagarfljót*: Robbie Robertson - *Somewhere Down the Crazy River*

6. The Northland

Pretty boring. Repetitive mountain/valley combo, little wild nature. You have to drive through it to get to the east (unless you take the

19

south route). Once you get east of *Akureyri*, things start looking up for the nature lover. Although not thought of as a fjords area, the northland is geographically heavily subdivided into fjords/bays, each with a corresponding valley or plains area and a regional capital. From west to east there's *Húnaflói* / *Blönduós, Skagafjörður* / *Sauðárkrókur, Eyjafjörður* / *Akureyri* and *Skjálfandi* / *Húsavík*. Throughout history, this was the most heavily populated area of Iceland until the ballooning urbanization of the *Reykjavík* area in the 20th century. *Akureyri* is the largest town outside the southwest and erstwhile rival for the status of capital city. It's too big to make it as a quaint village, and too small to be a city. North of there you'll find the old seaport *Gásir*. They make a big deal of history there so you might take a look at what's cooking. *Hrísey* is an increasingly popular destination, a lovely village on an island that makes the *Sound of Music* look like steampunk. Perhaps the most exciting thing in this whole area is *Drangey*, an inaccessible, uninhabited island that was refuge to one of the major outlaws of the period (*Grettis saga*) who even swam the ocean to get there. If you can do that, you may consider yourself tough. Don't try it though - you'll get terminal Shrinkage. The sagas attest *Grettir* was small going in. (They do!)

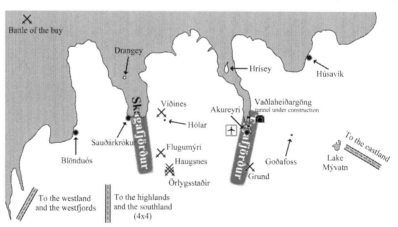

The Northland

The old Bishopric of the North had its seat at *Hólar*, worth a look maybe. Most of the fighting of the civil war period (see chapter 2) went down in the north, specifically in *Skagafjörður*. The most pivotal battle took place at *Örlygsstaðir*, decimating the powerful *Sturlungar* clan. The bloodiest battle was fought at *Haugsnes*. A chieftain famously survived fire and stabbings by hiding in a vat at *Flugumýri*. At *Víðines* the delinquent Bishop of the North (*Guðmundur the Good* - an early example of a leader of the Angela Merkel type - look him up) emerged victorious when the local warlord-poet was hit on the head with a rock. A wholly unexpected naval battle was fought off *Húnaflói* bay - probably the northernmost naval battle in history until WW2. Two fleets from different clans met by accident, each intending to invade the other's territory. In *Eyjafjörður* is located the homestead *Grund*. It is significant as the estate of the main branch of the *Sturlungar* clan,[6] and later the site of the slaying of the Norwegian governor/tax collector.

• Music suggestion for when *Akureyri* comes into view: Simple Minds - *Come a Long Way*

7. The Westfjords

It has fjords. It also has mountains, and between the mountains, sea. That is what we call fjords. If you like fjords, this is your Graceland, and Elvis is still alive. This area puts the *err...* in Terrible Roads, see chapter 5. The biggest town is *Ísafjörður*, yep, that means Icy Fjord. As if you needed reminding, on the Arctic's doorstep. Not much else is there, only some 7000 people live in this entire humongous area. It's connected to the mainland by a narrow isthmus.[7] You may not be surprised to learn that this area has historically been the tough

---

[6] The sagas claim the chieftain was so wealthy that he once fed the entire valley at his own expense through a hard year, and was not burdened by it - Iceland only became a shitty country later.

[7] My plan is to evacuate this area and turn it into a penal colony serving the whole of Europe. Then we can have reality TV shows modelled on *The Running Man* and *Escape From New York*. Once again, nobody listens to me.

end of Iceland. Don't get me wrong, things were rough all over, but nowhere rougher than here. Not a lot happened here, and most of it bad. The setting of *Gísla saga* (see below) is here, with the last stand at *Geirþjófsfjörður*. Gísli could have been a Hollywood hero (de Palma's *Scarface*?). During the civil war these fjords were a bitter bone of contention between two powerful outsider clans, to the degree that *Westfjordish sustenance* became a euphemism for

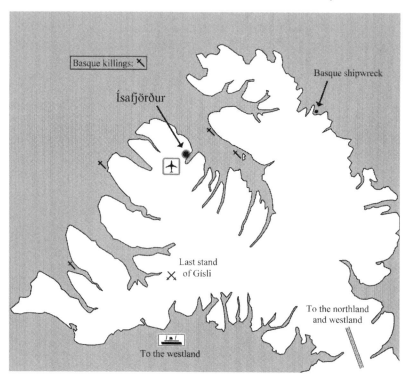

The Westfjords

plundering your neighbors. In the early 17th century, events equally bizarre and terrible hit the Westfjords. Basque whalers, evicted from Labrador, arrived to do their thing. Their activity was immediately banned by royal decree. When they were shipwrecked the 80-some survivors did some burglaring and were promptly declared outlaws by the local authority, hunted throughout the area and killed, sometimes gruesomely. This, the *Spanish Massacre* of 1615, is difficult to explain and certainly not for me to excuse, but the hardness of nature is known to harden the hearts of men. An exceptionally hard year, the locals were in a desperate situation following a failed summer. If you were facing starvation and uninvited strangers were roaming the neighborhood, plundering foodstuffs, even you, good-natured tourist, might soon discover what you are capable of.

Only recommended for the rugged outdoorsperson or hardcore surfer.

• Music suggestion when looking at the fjords and thinking about surfing them but not actually doing it: Beach Boys - *Surfin' USA*

8. The Westland

Now, this is my favorite area, but I suppose it's futile to ask you to stay out, so here goes:

The most cartoonish character of all that appear in the sagas, *Egill Skallagrímsson* (see chapter 3), had his homestead at *Borg*, near the modern town of *Borgarnes*, a beautiful town and popular stop. Only a few of his outrages occurred there, however. *Eiríkur the Red* was driven out of Norway on account of his killings. He made his homestead in the *Dales* at *Eiríksstaðir*. After also killing all too many people around his new home he was outlawed, and left to become the official discoverer of Greenland.[8] Also in the *Dales* was the original homestead of the *Sturlungar* clan at *Hvammur*. The most important Westlander is with little doubt *Snorri Sturluson* (see chapters 2 and 3). His castle stood at *Reykholt*, now a museum, complete with Snorri's original jacuzzi, fed geothermally. If you visit just one museum in Iceland, make it that one. Further up that valley, stop by some spectacular waterfalls (*Barnafoss*); don't try to

---

[8]Today a guy like this would be in prison. One wonders how many countries lie undiscovered because of it.

cross on the stone arch. The last idiot who tried fell in. Still further you'll find *Húsafell*, a beautiful recreational area, where the sun will come down on you like a hammer on a good day. You know that peninsula, that juts out from the west coast and is entirely too long and craggy? *Snæfellsnes*, they call it. For one thing it was home to a true-blooded serial killer, *Björn* from *Öxl*. Travellers used not to get further than his place, with robbery the motive. He had his head cut off; his son and grandson were both hanged for later misdeeds, so it seems the apple doesn't fall far from the bastard in Iceland. If you visit *Snæfellsnes* you'll meet aliens. But don't make a big fuss about it, they don't like it. You think they chose to land at *Snæfellsjökull* (it's where God dropped His ice cream) to talk to tourists? Think again. Anyway, this peninsula is craggy, did I mention already? Lots of interesting features to look at, and lots of birds. It even has a place called *Birdshit Cove* (*Dritvík*). Check out the Gangster Birds

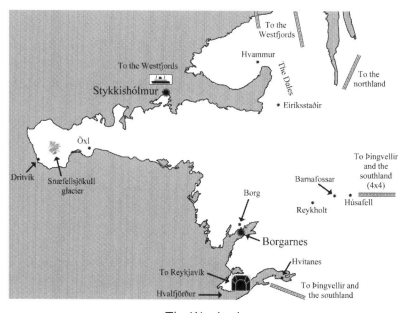

The Westland

24

while you're there. Also, skip the tunnel and go the long way, (route 47) a fantastic, mostly forgotten road around if not the longest, then certainly the best, fjord in Iceland, *Hvalfjörður*. Take it slow. It's almost as dangerous as it is beautiful, certified by *Top Gear* as one of the best driving roads in the world. It has many interesting stops along the way. At *Hvítanes* you can make out the ruins of a British WW2 naval installation, including the only remains of a railroad in Iceland (a rail pier). The entire fjord was an important allied base and a marshalling are for Russia-bound convoys, including the ill-fated PQ17. A shortcut through to *Þingvellir* and the southland is available. You don't want to end up in Reykjavík anyway.

• Music sugg. for the deep of *Hvalfjörður*: The Cult - *She Sells Sanctuary*

9. The Westmans

South of the southland you find the Westman Islands (don't ask). They are notable for volcanic activity under one's bed, puffins, and the *Festival of Drunken Sex* (see below). You can get there by plane or ferry. This archipelago has one inhabited island, *Heimaey*, and one newly created by volcanism in the 60's, *Surtsey*. The two most traumatizing historical events here are: *Tyrkjaránið* (1627) was a raid by Algerian corsairs who killed and captured a large proportion of the inhabitants. The *Heimaey* eruption (1973) almost wiped out the island and forced a complete evacuation. It's still hot.

• Music suggestion: Arthur Brown - *Fire*

10. The Highlands

The major chunk of inland area above roughly 500 meters elevation is beyond habitation or sustainable survival. It's a desert, mostly devoid of multicellular life, not counting tourists. What it has is rocks, glaciers, volcanoes and - you guessed it - geological features. It has a few major attractions such as *Landmannalaugar*, a geothermal area of natural beauty, and *Askja*, a large volcanic crater lake. An entire scientific expedition has disappeared in that lake without a trace or explanation, just so you know (so we'll call it the *Lake of Death* - also see chapter 2). Some roads run through the highlands, but they're bad. Enter at own foolhardiness - and NOT in your rental unless allowed - see chapter 6.

• Music suggestion: *Rawhide* theme

[Youtube: "Idiots in Iceland - locations playlist"]

So much for the locations, but how to get there? Iceland has roads, and where you're going, you need roads. The best known is the *Ringroad*, some 1400 km of mostly single carriageway metalled road that circles the country, i.e. the main body. It does not encompass peninsulas and such. Note that this is not a superhighway. Driving from one end of the country to the other takes pretty much the whole day. If you want to plan a day trip, don't go further than, say, 200 km. Lots of other roads are metalled, but many are not. If you want to get from one town to the next, all you need is your basic rental car. Driving is on the right, and all cars have the steering wheel on the left side. If you want to go deep, you probably need a big 4x4. Check your insurance conditions first. See chapters 5 - 6.

Domestic flights are available between *Reykjavík* and a few other towns. This is one route to the *Westmans*, the other being by ferry.

Some towns have local bus systems, notably Reykjavík and surroundings. Long distance bussing is available too. See Appendix B.

If you're waiting for the train, sit right down on the bench, next to the skeleton. There are no railways. See chapter 2.

Cycling on rural highways is a travel method chosen by some - but not by locals, that should tell you something. I'd say it's only for the really tough, hardcore cyclist, think Chuck Norris in tights. Iceland is a really bad country for cycling of this kind. It's windy, often cold even in summer, frequent showers, and roads tend to go up and down hills a lot. This is not the Rhineland. Think twice. However, if you enjoy torturing yourself, this is a good way, or at least a way, to combine that hobby with other enjoyable experiences. The Southland is Recommended for this activity, few hills, still weather and a dense road network. Down there it might not be torture after all.

How to pay for all this? Virtually all shops accept major credit cards. Only a few accept international currency. So, card or krónur. 100 krónur is worth somewhat less than a dollar, pound or euro at the time of writing. See Appendix B.

Before you go out there, be advised that Iceland is tough. It may be a magical land, but it's not Disneyland. It is not planned and landscaped for your convenience or safety (although it is without alligators). You'll hear a lot more on this subject in later chapters, but for now make sure you have sensible shoes, decent clothes, your brain plugged in and turned on and watch your step. If you are a reality-divorced suburbanite, try to imagine you are somebody else, like Clint Eastwood or Genghis Khan or Dian Fossey or Bear Grylls (I can't believe I mentioned HIM). What would they do? Would Clint Eastwood try to ford a river in a *Yaris*? Would Genghis Khan allow himself to swept off his feet by ocean waves? Would Dian Fossey go caving in high heels? Okay, forget Bear Grylls, he'd do all of those things.

The Lowdown on the Locals

Apart from geology, the human presence in Iceland may be an object of interest. Starting from the top, the **New Year** is celebrated with an excess of fireworks. It is something they're big on in this place. Excess that is. It's the only way to be. After that the locals try to enjoy their annual bout of depression (seasonal affective disorder), the next time you see them (or want to see them anyway) is in March. However, they're genetically modified. Icelanders are about half as likely to suffer mental problems from prolonged darkness as anybody else. It's evolution stupid! Survival of the fittest. They've been locked in this place for over a thousand years with no escape route. Those who didn't dig the dark... well they didn't do too well. It's you who are the risk group. If you do stay here through January-February, keep tabs on your mental state. Are you thinking altogether too much about eating your grandmother? Then take a step back, time for a reality check. You'll get better from March onward.

Easter is a somewhat big deal, for most people it's a 5 day weekend, and an even longer spring break for students. Local Easter eggs are excessively large (did you guess?), up to three pounds. Really. That's including a generous filling of assorted candy, like a chocolate piñata. (*It was The Easter Bunny... in the Study.... with The Easter Egg*). This way the locals are guaranteed something comforting to munch on while contemplating the Passion.

The **national holiday** is June 17 and is only celebrated in the rain. It's actually the only day of the year when you'll find more locals than tourists on the streets of Reykjavík city centre - unless Iceland wins (or doesn't lose big) at a football tournament.

The summer brings a raft of **local festivals** and celebrations of various strange concepts (see Appendix D), for example in the northernmost north (*Siglufjörður*) there's the *Festival of Salted Herring*. There, herring can be encountered in both salted and pre-salted form. Then there is the (countrywide) *Festival of Drunken Sex* at the beginning of August. This festival puts the *Bin* in Binge Drinking (the one you vomit into). Also there's music. This is nowhere more rigorously celebrated than in the Westmans, where it is supposedly the national holiday. Go figure.

Christmas starts in October and is celebrated with..... I knew you'd get it - excess! They're really big on Christmas here, mainly because it's a no-brainer opportunity to indulge in excess. Knock on any door at 18:00 on December 24 and you'll get presents, food and drink. Don't do it though. The period from then until New Year's and technically until January 6 is a non-stop feast of materialistic indulgence. It's their way of reminding themselves of the birth of Jesus Christ and his message to the world. There were even nine santas. (They're brothers, and their mother eats babies, see chapter 3) That turned out not to be enough, so the total was brought up to thirteen, and they all bring presents. But they also steal, vandalise, interfere with farm animals, and make various malicious practical jokes and if you ask them, coke is not it. Welcome to Iceland.

Today, the **population** is something like 340.000. That makes Sweden 30 times larger and the United States 1000 times larger. About 10% of that number is foreign-born, mostly East European. If you include sheep in the total, and why not, it goes up to half a million.

Almost all Icelanders speak fairly good or even fluent **English**. Other foreign languages, not so well. If your English is OK, you'll be OK. If not, you're in trouble.

Something foreigners notice is that Icelanders don't use hankies or blow their noses; not to put a too fine point on it, they suck it up. Now, I'm not here to make excuses, but factor in perhaps that in this climate, blowing your nose would make for A LOT of dirty hankies. Also note, table manners may be borderline.

Iceland is a traditional parliamentary democracy. The parliament, *Alþingi*, has a single camera of 63 seats, elected proportionally from six constituencies. The most influential political party is the Conservative Party (*Sjálfstæðisflokkurinn*). Social Democrats are traditionally weak and fragmented in Iceland, unusually for Scandinavia. A President with limited powers is elected by popular vote, and is traditionally free of overt party affiliation.

Iceland has no air force, no army and no navy. The only institution with a military tradition is the Coast Guard, who defeated the British Navy in the *Cod Wars*. Weapons were not used in those wars, or they might conceivably have had a different outcome (see ch. 2).

What if you want to compare the locals to something else, something you know? I'll give that a try. The core scandis - Norway, Denmark, Sweden - perhaps you have a feel for them. Icelanders are more individualistic than they are, more nationalistic, more crude, and perhaps less overall scandi-like, although this is changing. The Icelander is historically more streetwise than the core scandis, but too much of a good thing in terms of prosperity is now eroding the Icelanders' common sense. Inasmuch as Finns are like Russians, I suppose Icelanders are like Americans. It's a shot in the dark, but it might hit the target. Norwegians and Swedes are more idealistic than Icelanders (their feet hardly seem to touch the ground from where we're sitting) but Danes are very well grounded, much better than Icelanders. In terms of cool factor, Icelanders come out pretty well I guess. It is hard to deny that they are a rather **cool** bunch, despite everything. Danes are **uncool** however,[9] and smoke too much. Swedes and Norwegians are **seriously uncool**. They are more square than an IKEA flatpack. Norwegians wouldn't know a joke if it stabbed them in the spleen, and you have to get a Swede drunk just to stop him boring you to death. Call it self-defense. Finns, on the other hand, are **cool**, bordering on **subzero**, even in silly trousers - and they have great jokes.[10] Us, we can't beat them, we're not even worthy. How can you hope to compete with people who have a restaurant with tractors as furniture? Since we are covering this whole field, what of the Faeroese? Well, you'd think they're a bit bland, being the ones who couldn't be bothered to make more than half the trip, but the opposite is true. They are perhaps like extreme Icelanders. They are in fact the only nation in the world that looks up to us and will lend us money without strings attached. It's nice to have friends. Still, it's just too easy to make fun of the Faeroese. Icelandic and Faeroese language are

---

[9] The internationally recognized Clarkson Scale of Coolness

[10] Do you know the Finnish game, Yukka? Several guys sit in the sauna and pass the vodka bottle. When the bottle is empty, they all draw their knives and throw them. The guy hit by the knives, he is Yukka.

pretty similar - they can just about understand one another. However, individual words often have different meanings or are formed in a way that seems nearly correct but idiotically modified, and a sentence in Faeroese frequently comes out to an Icelander as really funny or even an outrageously ludicrous or smutty joke only a total jerk could come up with (the author resisted the temptation to print one). The converse is also true, apparently.

Icelanders like new things - A LOT. They want to own all the latest gadgets. As early as the year 2000, meaningful existence in Iceland without a mobile phone had become impossible.

PC is not big with the Icelander, in fact meat products from the *SS* are widely available. Further, Icelanders are incoherent, they change their mind easily, especially when money enters the picture and are given to hysterics for little cause. That's mostly because they feel thinking comes after speaking. They mostly follow rules when it suits them, in sharp contrast to say, Germans or English (see chapter 2). They have a decision aversion, they like to postpone decisions until the last moment, whenever possible. They are not very fond of planning, playing it by ear is preferred. Details don't interest them much. Neither do principles. If it works, it's good. If it's unsound, unethical or even criminal, that's just aggregate.

Sounds pretty bad, all this. A pretty exasperating bunch to work with, one would expect. Is there even an upside? There is, as it happens. If you're looking for a crew to work fast and effectively under pressure, to improvise, or in a crisis situation, look no further. When the volcano opened up almost inside the town in Heimaey in the middle of the night, they got everybody (5300 people) off the island in 6 hours with no injuries. When the quake struck Haiti in 2010, the Icelandic team was there running an operation within 24 hours - while everybody else was putting their boots on. And if you need a crack team of unconventional accountants to urgently cut through the red tape - *what* red tape? Just don't let them run an investment bank - the horror...

There's a high degree of trust and camaraderie in Icelandic society, coupled with a sense of unity of purpose. Whether these conditions survive for much longer in a global environment, who knows.

Nature and Lack Thereof

In terms of **vegetation**, Iceland today is mostly a desert or near-desert. The aboriginal forest, which was birchwood and not very tall, was destroyed since human occupation through the production of charcoal. Also, wild roaming sheep to this day ensure that the forest doesn't grow back. They may look all sweet, innocent and wooly, but believe me, they're evil! Reforestation efforts today are mainly based on imported evergreens such as pine and fir. They are sheepproof. Also, the crassly blue plants seen everywhere are Alaskan Lupins, introduced for their soil generating potential. They have become a highly contentious issue, but it is pretty clear by now that they're not going away anytime soon. Edible berries are in season from late July. These are blueberries, and the smaller *Krækiber* (Crowberry) which are black. Could be confused with caviar from a distance. Blueberries are more highly prized, but then again you can get any number of blueberry products from the shops, but nothing with Crowberry. The latter go great with Skyr. Also, Crowberries contain a high proportion of aggregate which accu-

Krækiber / Crowberry

A foxy Fox

mulates in your mouth. A popular sport is that when you've eaten a lot of them you spit the aggregate in the next person's face. You didn't hear it from me though. In terms of wild **fauna**, there's not much to shock the traveller. There's the arctic fox (the only aboriginal land vertebrate) and some mice. Very occasionally there are visits by polar bears, but not to worry, they are shot as soon as they make their presence known.

Introduced species include reindeer; they can annoy because they seem to think they own the highways, and refuse to give way. They mostly hang out in the eastern highlands, fortunately. If you want to shoot one, there's a free lottery for licences - anyone can join! Only... not through a car window, please. Then there's introduced American Mink, long considered a pest. The semi-wild sheep population is also a pest, as far as this author is concerned. There's loads of horses (80.000+), the pony-like, five-gaited Icelandic breed. Importation of livestock (and pets) is illegal (disease control), and take note horse lovers: importation of used paraphernalia such as saddles, reins etc. is also illegal and viewed very seriously. There are no reptiles. So, no snakes.

Horsie

An Sheep

Insects are fairly benign. No poisonous spiders; no scorpions; and can you belive, Greenland has them and so does the Kola peninsula, but here - no mosquitos! There are woodticks that can give you Lyme's disease, but rare. Tiny flies, *Mý*, do suck blood and are highly annoying and very not rare, but do not spread disease. Known to induce temporary insanity in forestry workers. They're timid and try to get into a safe place to suck, up your sleeve or in your ear canal. If one is trespassing around your ear, beat it off fast! If it gets in, pour water in the ear canal. If you find one on your arm, already sucking away, you can pinch its wings and pull it backwards. That way the tube doesn't break off and infect the wound. In any case, the bite irritates only slightly. There's a popular destination in the northeast, a lake called *Mývatn* - guess what you'll find there!

Iceland has **birds**. A lot of birds. Very possibly a thousand birds for every human. The best loved by locals is not the one you think, it's the *Golden Plover* (*Heiðlóa/Lóa*). It's a migratory bird which arrives in March. Its distinctive call signals that spring is just around the corner. This means so much to the Icelander

Heiðlóa / Golden Plover

Kría / Gangster bird

Lundi / Puffin

that the earliest captured recording of the *Lóa's* song is sometimes played over the radio. Ahhhh... the joy! There's one bird however that's hard to love, the *Fulmar* or *Skunk Bird* (*Fýll*). It looks like something between a gull and an Albatross. If you get too close it will vomit a disgusting liquid all over you. Fortunately it doesn't get in your way, it only stays in high cliffs. Of all Icelandic birds, the *Atlantic Puffin* (Lundi) is the most famous, and the silliest. It looks like an alcoholic butler, and flies like an obese person running the 100 meter dash. That said, it's damn cute. What is not cute, is the *Tern* (*Kría*). It looks like a gangster, and if you see them flocking, try walking over there. Be warned, if you do you'll get a surprise. Hint: Alfred Hitchcock.

Let me describe the **weather** in Iceland in general terms, for the pedestrian tourist - if you are the outdoors tooth-and-nail type, re- fer to chapter 5. First of all, it's not that cold! Especially in the southwest, winters are mild. They hardly see snow there anymore, although they used to, some 30 years ago. You can expect temper- atures to bounce between $-5°C$ and $+5°C$ in the winter. What is going to bother you most is the wind; chilly, wet, unrelenting. In the north and east you can expect more still weather, colder bouts of some duration, and sometimes persistent, thick snow. Only a few years ago a freak storm blanketed the northeast with several meters of snow in september. They were digging the sheep out for weeks afterwards, in many cases even alive - although bored. But that was a freak. The kind of deep cold, under $-20°C$ for extended periods like you get in Sweden and Finland, that is not commonplace, and virtually unheard of in the southwest. The summers are not hot. They can be slow in starting, the first half of June is often exas- perating, alternating between wind, rain, and wind and rain at the same time. Once in a while you even get a non-starter summer in the southwest. Again, the north and east are different, with higher likelihood of fine weather. In a good summer you'll get something like $+15°C$ to $+20°C$ or more in July, it is very pleasant and usually you have just the right breeze to go with it so it doesn't get oppressive. In the southland you can get heavy stills with difficulty sleeping at night. The eastland usually gets the temperature records in summer, almost a continental climate. The weather is generally very changeable in Iceland, never the same two days in a row or so they say. This appears to be changing in recent years, with more uniformity linked to certain climate phenomena. You, as a mobile tourist, can take advantage of the fact that when the weather is bad in the southwest it is usually good in the northeast - and vice versa - and now a certain persistence in weather patterns. Therefore, be advised to keep your plans fluid and **chase the sun**. That's what I might put my money on in your position.

Iceland is the #1 beneficiary of the Gulf Stream - the steady, warm ocean current that originates in the Gulf of Mexico. Therefore it's a lot warmer than the longitude indicates. The landmass is a product of a major rift in the Atlantic Ridge, which keeps drifting apart. Volcanism keeps filling the gap. The valley of *Þingvellir* is a classic rift valley, with fissures at each side. The geologic age is less than 20 million years. That, combined with isolation, makes for a lack of biodiversity. Iceland is a major beneficiary of Global Warming. The climate has improved considerably in the last 25 years or so, and could improve further. Fish stocks, such as Macrel, have moved north into Icelandic waters, yielding serious extra revenue (the Europeans are not happy about it). Even the melting of glaciers would be a short term benefit. If the Greenland ice sheet melts, world sea level would rise by up to 7 meters. However, because of the gravitational attraction of the ice mass, its removal would actually lower the sea level of the immediate area, including Icelandic waters. Bring it on!

Alcohol, Tobacco and Firearms

Icelanders have a traditionally fraught relationship with **alcohol**. The earliest drink was mead, brewed from honey. Since distillation was introduced, the traditional drink has been a version of Aquavitae, *Brennivín* (literally 'Burning Wine') today brewed from Caraway, which soon gained a dark reputation. So dark that it was only allowed to be sold under a pitch black and uninviting label.[11] Total prohibition entered into force in 1915, but was repealed for wine in 1922 (Iberians, see chapter 2), for spirits in 1935 and for beer in 1989 (you heard me). The Icelandic drinking model is basically binge drinking on weekends. Drinking on or before a working day is considered abnormal, apart from occasionally having one beer after work or a glass of wine with dinner. The after-work-pint tradition is nonexistent. Being touched while on the clock would be highly irregular. Drinking until you vomit in a wardrobe and pass out on a saturday night is considered normal, however. Alcoholism has traditionally been a major social problem, and alcohol related illnesses major health problems - although not including cirrhosis of the liver, which mainly affects drinkers who never dry out during the week, i.e. your cultured, evening drinker. You see, people have a real downer on binge drinking, but it has several upsides compared with daily wine drinking. A binge culture usually consumes a smaller total amount than a daily wine one. The consumers are mostly dry during the week, so they are better workers and safer drivers. Liver disease - see above. Downsides are injuries, brain damage and other misfortunes while smashed. And don't tell me about Russia, it's a special case. If you were Ivan Q Public in Russia, you'd want to be drunk all the time too. Btw drinking culture is a function of climate. Cold climate - bingeing; warm climate - daily drinking. Some countries (the goldilocks principle) have the best of both worlds (like England) - binge on weekends AND drink culturally during the week.

The sale of alcohol is strictly regulated. Apart from licensed restaurants and bars, alcohol (including wine and beer) can ONLY be bought at government monopoly stores (*Vínbúðin*). Not to worry,

---

[11]Yep, we invented that - and have known for longer than anybody else that it doesn't work.

they are thick on the ground and offer pretty good variety. Alcohol is heavily taxed (up to 550% not including markup) and thus expensive. The taxation gives rise to a weird price structure, as it is largely the spirit content that is taxed. Therefore the finest 12-year whiskey costs just fractionally more than trash bourbon. So drink in style while in Iceland. No points for figuring out that there's a great financial incentive to shop for alcohol at Duty Free on your way in. There is a limit to what each person can bring in (ask - I will not risk inaccurate info on this). You must be 20 years old to legally buy, possess or drink alcohol. Handing even a beer to someone who is 19 and a half is a crime. Have your credentials on hand when buying.

VÍNBÚÐIN
Áfengis- og tóbaksverslun ríkisins

DUI is illegal, obviously (> 0,25% blood alcohol level) and is punishable by a fine and loss of licence. Jail time for repeat offenders. Note that bicycling under the influence is treated identically!

Smoking is no longer cool in Iceland, and has been on a long decline. Tobacco is regulated by the same authority as alcohol, yet can be bought from regular shops. It is heavily taxed and expensive. The age limit for buying is 18 years.

Icelanders have a lot of **guns**. What for, you ask? Well, shooting. Hunting and sport that is. Legal civilian gun ownership accounts for maybe 90.000 weapons (almost all longarms), which works out at roughly one gun per household. Gun homicides since the turn of the century come to the grand total of two, if not counting that the police lit up some nutter a couple of years ago. There is also a considerable number of illegal firearms out there, including handguns. Most criminals of note pack heat, but never use it. Interestingly, a few years ago a drug deal went sour in Reykjavík and some thug did pull out a shotgun and started blasting away. Nobody was hit. The police jumped on the guy with both feet, and all the other criminals lined up against this individual and let it be known in no uncertain terms that this kind of behaviour was not favored. It turns out the criminal underworld is strongly anti-gun (or anti-shooting anyway). The police carry guns, but not openly. The commando unit has handguns, rifles and machineguns. Regular police cars contain handguns in a locker, but officers need clearance to use them. Conclusion? I guess guns don't kill people, at least not in Iceland. An statistic: If there was only one gun in Iceland, you'd have to wait nearly one million years for the first gun homicide. In the US you'd only have to wait 30.000 years for someone to be blown away.

Culinary Specialties

You may already have heard that Iceland has a long tradition of renowned dishes of delicacy. In that case you heard wrong. There are some local specialty foods that you don't need to run away from, but also several you should.

Skyr: Milk pudding somewhat similar to yoghurt, but thicker. Recommended for breakfast, perhaps mixed with cereal and milk. Available everywhere in a staggering variety of flavors. Hint: berries are in season from late July. Go out with a couple of tubs of skyr (plain, vanilla or coconut flavor), find some Crowberries (see the nature section), shovel them into your skyr and eat it up with a spoon. Don't bother with blueberry, you can buy blueberry flavored skyr at the shop. Btw I realize that skyr is now available all over the world, but we invented it, it's ours, like *Feta* is Greek.

Graflax: This is like sushi, only 5 times better. This is uncooked but cured and seasoned salmon. The original treatment back in the day was to bury the salmon in the ground for an extended period. What they do with it today I don't know. I do know it tastes like a million krónur. Don't confuse with smoked salmon, which is less good. Thin slices on bread, preferably toast, with special graflax sauce - and this is my personal secret ingredient I will tell you alone - some lumpfish caviar on top of that. Recommended. In fact, I'm going to have some right now.

Whale meat: Can you imagine the tenderest of tenderloin beef steak? That is not as tender as properly cooked whale steak. 'Properly' is the key word here, because it's tricky. Whale meat is easily ruined, and not only from guilt. The thing is, if you cook it slowly by any means whatsoever, it turns grey, tasteless and tough as leather, the culinary equivalent of a turd in a swimming pool. Likewise you can't reheat it, but there's nothing wrong with eating it cold. The thing to do is to cut thin slices, about half a centimeter, get your frying pan as hot as you can, use lots of oil in the pan and preferably pre-oil the slices. When the pan is hot enough to burn a hole in the space-time continuum, smack those slices in there for 30 seconds, turn them, and after another 30 seconds pull them out. This is not a job for the naked chef, as drops of searing hot oil fly everywhere. Wear long sleeves and set your fume extractor to warp speed. Don't skimp on the spices, lemon pepper is favored. Fresh is preferable to frozen, because the latter acquires a slight oily tinge. If ordering in a restaurant, be firm in asking if the meat is fresh or frozen. Recommended. However, PCBs and Mercury accumulate in such a long-lived animal; therefore don't have it everyday, only eat the meat (not blubber) and best abstain if you're pregnant.[12]

All right, I can sense what you're thinking, so let's get this out of the way. Iceland hunts two species of whale. One is *Hrefna* (Minke), a small rorqual that numbers some 180.000 in the North Atlantic and is not threatened in any way ('Least Concern'). The other is *Langreyður* (Fin), a larger rorqual that is listed as endangered on a worldwide basis. That's misleading however, as the Fin exists in several population groups. The population in the southern ocean is most threatened, whereas in the Iceland area they do not seem to have suffered more than a modest decline in numbers since hunting

---

[12] Incidentally, the Icelandic word *Hvalreki*, literally *Whale drift*, means a dead whale washed up on the shore. It signifies a huge and unexpected bonus. Back in the day such an occurrence could mean the difference between life and death for lowly farmers and was sometimes bitterly fought over.

began. The Greenland-Norway gap alone is estimated to have more than 10.000 Fins. Look it up if you don't believe me. Then have a guilt free whale steak, or at least don't bitch about it if I do.

<u>Shark</u>: If you must, but not on my account. Hold your nose and think of George Clooney. A shot of brennivín helps it go down smoothly. That should tell you something.

<u>Skate</u>: There is a tradition to feast on this awful insult to senses (and sense) on December 23 each year. It actually makes your eyes water, by just being in the same room. Originally, the masters served this dish from hell to the household so as to guarantee that whatever they served up for Christmas dinner on the next day would taste good in comparison (this is true, from the highest authority). I.e. skate was intentionally served as the worst tasting food in Iceland, and that's saying something. Today there's no such dilemma, there's no shortage of good food for Christmas. Yet people continue this perverted ritual, even going so far as to convince themselves that it actually tastes good. The limits of self-delusion are wide indeed. Put on your best running shoes - tell them you have to return some videotapes. If you do smell something not even remotely funny on the 23rd, know it is not a terrorist chemical attack.

<u>Þorra-food</u>: This is another silly tradition, taking place in January, or in the month of Þorri by the old calendar. People gather in large groups (Þorrablót) to feast on shit, really. In olden days in the dead of winter, people would eat a lot of unsavory things to stay alive. Examples of Þorra-dishes include shark, pickled rams' testicles, roasted sheep's faces, whale blubber, pickled fish maw, black pudding, haggis (unseasoned), pig jelly, sheep jelly, seals' fins etc. And no, this is not a scene from Life of Brian. People still want to do this, even though this country is now a horn o'plenty. I forgot to mention one dish though... it's Brennivín in major quantity. That might explain the popularity. "Þorramatur" therefore is a synonym for weird, unusual and/or disgusting food you would not normally

touch and are best off running away from. Avoid. See Appendix A.

Horse sausage: This is a large, chunky sausage, foot-long or more, containing (ideally) coarsely ground horsemeat. The sausage is often packaged in a horseshoe shape. Look for the words *Grófhökkuð hrossabjúgu* on the wrapping. Important: puncture the sheath before cooking. Boil for 90 minutes. Eat up, preferably with mashed potato. Pick out the fatty bits with a fork. You'll never use the phrase *I could eat a horse* in vain again. Acquired taste. Also a handy weapon for home protection. *It's all right officer, the intruder has been schlonged!*

Fish: What can I say other than *A LOT*? A lot of fish, a lot of variety, cheap, and very fresh - and let's face it, you probably don't even know what fresh fish is. If you have access to cooking facilities, visit a fish shop and go crazy. Break out the recipe book or borrow an internet. Listen, if you are a Vegan or something like that, this is your chance to crack. Have you started suffering from memory problems? Do you need a calculator to add two-digit numbers? Your brain needs fat, and there's no better fat than fish fat. You can tell your friends on the collective farm that burly animal-haters kidnapped you and forced it down your throat, and of course you hated every filthy piece of it.

Dried fish: This is called *Harðfiskur* (Hardfish) and is considered a delicacy. It is very expensive by weight, but keep in mind how that calculation turns out when all the water has been removed. This is ideal for the hardy outdoorsperson, very light and nutritious and can be consumed straight up, even while hiking. A pinch of butter is favored on your *Harðfiskur*. Not intended for rehydrating btw.

Brennivín/snow pudding: This is my personal invention, and I'll share it with you alone. Take a typical glass, ideally a whiskey glass with straight vertical sides. Fill it 40% up with Brennivín. Then take it outside and cram fresh fallen snow into the glass until it's full and the contents have the texture of pudding. Eat with a teaspoon at your leisure, it melts only very slowly. Perfect for a skiing holiday, everyone will become interested in you. Note that this only works with fresh snow or you'll end up with Brennivín Crush.

Lamb: This is the crowning glory of Icelandic cuisine. Ok, I'm not going giddy, but I'll tell you this: If you have tried lamb before, but not Icelandic lamb, then you haven't actually tried lamb at all. The difference is that here the lamb enjoys a wild existence through the summer with lots of excercise and exotic diet before it is killed with great compassion. Maybe. That really delivers in the taste. Great for BBQ. Only, while you're chewing, reflect on the fact that you are subsidising the ongoing destruction of Icelandic Flora.

Lýsi: A fish oil produce. In terms of vitamins, this is a WMD. A pillar of Icelandic health through the ages, especially in winter. Have a fruity drink on hand to wash it down, it has an aftertaste from hell. If you are a Vegan, I expect this would do you a world of good. Mind your intake, this is not for gulping down.

Hot Dogs: The locals seem to think these are the bee's knees, but I have never understood why. They are not made from quality ingredients. You will probably try one, but don't expect much.

Vegetables: You've come to the wrong country.

Film and TV

This author chooses to believe that to every nation belongs a film that embodies the soul of that nation. For the English, it's *The Italian Job*, to name an example. For the Dutch, it's *The Flodders* (maybe) to name another. In the unlikely event that you want to get inside Icelanders' heads, perhaps the quickest start to such a journey of discovery is through local films and TV. It's mostly rubbish, but there are some titles out there that are not only good but can be said to represent the national character in some way or another - or are at least loved by the typical Icelander.

• *Blóðrautt sólarlag* (The Crimson Sunset) (1977) - Early horror feature. Little gore, but lingering fear throughout. B&W. • IMDB: 7.0.

• *Útlaginn* (Outlaw - The Saga of Gísli) (1981) - A faithful presentation of one of the ancient sagas, somewhat neatly done. Unmissable to the historically minded. • IMDB: 6.5.

• *Með allt á hreinu* (On Top) (1982) - A musical film; searching for that Big Break. The humor is perhaps a little too quaint for the metropolitan tourist, but the slightly older generation of Icelanders love it. T'was the previos soul film, before Sódóma. Not recommended. So why did I mention it? Who can tell? Do you know the reasons for everything you do? • IMDB: 7.4.

• *Rokk í Reykjavík* (Rock in Reykjavík) (1982) - Musical documentary covering especially the Punk Rock scene, which was pretty colorful. Includes Björk at 16. • IMDB: 7.3.

• *Hrafninn flýgur* (When the Raven Flies / Revenge of the Barbarians) (1984) - Cheesy, Spaghetti-Western style, ahistorical Viking drama/action thriller. Wait for that guy to say: "Heavy knife". A sequel exists. • IMDB: 6.8.

• *Sódóma Reykjavík* (Remote Control) (1992) - A ludicrous comedy, this film is the soul film as per previous comments. A young man scours Reykjavík to procure a replacement for his mother's lost TV remote. Other things happen too. Contains the best one-liner in history. Major contemporary musical talents act and/or perform. Recommended. • IMDB: 7.9.

• *Limbó* (1993) - Comedy sketch show and sitcom of edgy humor. Edgy enough that it was cancelled after only two episodes. It was just too raunchy for those times. Translation may not be available. See Appendix A. • IMDB: 8.1.

• *Fóstbræður* (1997 - 2001) - Comedy sketch TV show of new wave humor. Sketches include: Let's kill grandpa, The towel of death, Zealous showers attendant, Helgi - the personal troubadour, The shoes of death, The taxi driver of death, Brunnhilde, The foot of death, The rude mum. Recommended. See Appendix A. • IMDB: 9.2.

• *Englar Alheimsins* (Angels of the Universe) (2000) - Funny yet serious story of four certified lunatics and the challenges they face in their lives - and the challenges they pose to other people. Enjoyable by all. Recommended. • IMDB: 7.7.

• *Næturvaktin* (Night Shift) (2007) - Sitcom set in a Reykjavík petrol station. Georg, the night manager, threatens the emotional well-being of his staff and customers with outrageous eccentricities and mental torture. See also two further seasons, *Dagvaktin* (Day Shift) and *Fangavaktin* (Prison Shift) and feature film, *Bjarnfreðarson*. Starring then-future mayor of Reykjavík, Jón Gnarr. Recommended. • IMDB: 8.8.

Yes all right, those IMDB scores don't have a huge number of votes behind them.

[Youtube: "Idiots in Iceland - film & TV"]

Popular Music

Ok I'll do my best here. Dates refer to first form. Frankly I think Icelandic music is a bit crap, but here goes:

• *Stuðmenn* - (1970) Phenomenally popular band, but never made it on the world stage. Co-wrote and feature in *Með allt á hreinu* (see above). • Suggested first listen: *Í bláum skugga*.

• *Þursaflokkurinn* - (1978) Folk themed prog rock band. • First listen: *Sigtryggur vann*. Acquired taste - Recommended.

• *Brunaliðið* - (1978) A middle of the road pop band. • First listen: *Ég er á leiðinni*.

• *HLH Flokkurinn* - (1978) Cooky Retro Pop. • First listen: *Riddari götunnar.*

• *Sykurmolarnir* / *The Sugarcubes* - (1986) Björk's first taste of world fame. Opened for U2. • First listen: *Regina.*

• *HAM* - (1988) Heavy metal band; opened for *Rammstein.* Appear as themselves in *Sódóma* (see above). Frontman *Sigurjón Kjartansson* has many talents. • First listen: *Partíbær.* Recommended.

• *Sigur Rós* - (1994) There was no getting around this. Just please try to remember we're not all mongoloids here. • First listen: *Olsen olsen.*

• *Botnleðja* - (1994) Grunge. Can you tell they were ripped off? • First listen: *Þið eruð frábær.*

• *Quarashi* - (1996) White Rappers. • First listen: *Baseline.* Check out the video, Cod Wars theme. Recommended.

• *Skálmöld* - (2009) Viking themed metal band. • First listen: *Kvaðning.*

[Youtube: "Idiots in Iceland - popular music playlist"]

2. A Brief History of Ice

To understand one's present situation, one must know history. You, an almost normal person, are now located in perhaps the strangest place in the world, which yet has toilets with running water. How did this come about? I promise I'll try not to be boring.

Habitation with intent began in Iceland in 874 AD if you belive the Skins (the ancient sagas, written on calf's skin), and you do. Settlers arrived by *Knörr*, the ocean-going ship type, distinct from the coast-bound *Longship*. The sagas also tell of Irish monks who were here before the norse, called *Papas*. Certainly, there were no *Mamas*. Anyway, they soon left, one way or another. Most male settlers came from Norway, but apparently the womenfolk were not terribly interested in joining. So to make up the gender shortfall the boys snatched some girls on the way, i.e. from Britain, only picking the prettiest ones. This is supposedly why certain genetic traits are found in Iceland (and vice versa). The first Pioneer (OK, I'm not much into namedropping but here goes) was *Ingólfur Arnarson*, and he was pretty smart or we can start believing in coincidence. He made his home in Reykjavík. It is the best place to live in Iceland, or at least it used to be. Then some other folks arrived and in short order, the country was full. 60.000 people in all and that's a lot for those times. Norway was only 180.000. This was before Keflavík Airport opened, which makes it even more amazing.

Those settlers soon founded the *Alþingi* (930), i.e. a parliament that made laws and sat in judgement of disputes and crimes, at *Þingvellir*. Thereby the Old Republic (or Commonwealth) was formed. There was no government or law enforcement organ - but as this began pre-writing, there was the crucial office of *Lawsayer* - one who each session would lay down the law as he knew it.[13] The courts were reliant on the people themselves to enforce decisions. In practice

---

[13] Not even Hollywood has this

the aggrieved party was given licence to do so, even violently. The *Alþingi* operated with diminishing relevance into the Time of Troubles / civil war, and under foreign rule with curtailed powers until final dissolution in 1800. Now, you may hear from proud locals or even international windbags that the *Alþingi* was the world's first parliament as we know it. I'm sorry, but anybody saying that, you have my permission to stamp on their foot and poke them in the eye (figuratively speaking, of course!), because it is indulgent nonsense. What it was, was actually an advanced form of pre-civilizational germanic democratic institution which by that time was dying out. The connection with modern parliamentary democracy on the English model (or indeed the present-day *Alþingi*) is absolutely none.

It's worth it to examine the term *Viking* and what it actually means. It's derived from *vík*, meaning an inlet, in the way that in Norway, fleets of marauders would take up temporary residence in fjords and inlets and plunder the inhabitants, then move on to the next. This proved an insurmountable challenge to authority, turning Norway into a failed state in the 10th century. The activities of these so-called *Sea Kings* are famous outside Scandinavia. The point is that the term is derogatory, not on a par with *Spear chucker* perhaps, but inappropriate as a description of a nation.

For a good while the Icelanders quite enjoyed being heathens, believing in a noble family clan of fallible gods (see chapter 3). Then it was decided by the EU.... I mean the King of Norway that this could not go on. He had just brought the message of love from Jesus to his own countrymen through an unprecedented campaign of murder, maiming and arson, and he was not going to tolerate a bunch of technically runaway Norwegians thinking otherwise - especially since the end of the world was scheduled for the year 1000 and time was running short. The thing about Icelanders is that they don't take religion (or anything, even) seriously, never have, and probably never will (doing so could even be described as *Unicelandic*). So, with this message from the King, which you can believe was a pretty serious one, (*Christianize, or else!*, also known as a *Hostile Makeover*), they asked the current Lawsayer, Þorgeir Ljósvetningagoði, what they should do and he thought about it - for all of three days. He decreed that there should be one law only, for if the law should be rent asunder, then so would the peace be. Therefore there could only be one religion for all. They took his advice, which was like, hey, let's all be Christians now and sod the old stuff. But if you have issues with letting go, you can actually keep doing that pagan shit you like, just as long as you do it under your own roof and nobody finds out, or there'll be hell to pay! Best solution ever. *Þorgeir* then added that *Solomon* could kiss his ass - possibly.

Around the same time *Leifur Eiríksson*, nicknamed *the Lucky*, discovered North America (*Vínland* - Newfoundland/New Brunswick; *Markland* - Labrador (?)) by accidentally sailing a gazillion miles too far southwest. I don't know why they didn't call him *the Incredibly Stupid*. Those lands are described in the sagas as extremely favorable, with wild grape and wheat and lots of lumber. Anyway, he was Icelandic. Don't listen to the Norwegians on this one, they are full of it. So there you have it, Icelanders discovered America 500 years before Colombo (not the detective). Not only that, they were smart enough to lose it again. It had Indians you see, and Leifur and his crew didn't have Winchesters. Some settlements were attempted (*L'Anse aux Meadows*) but abandoned within a relatively short time. In the meantime, the first Christian was born in America - if that means something.

It was actually Leifur's father *Eiríkur* nicknamed *the Red* who discovered Greenland a couple of decades earlier (Lots of discoverin' in that family). He killed somebody he shouldn't have and was outlawed, so he sailed into the west on the strength of mariners' tales. He came back and presented his find as a land greener than green itself.[14] He never mentioned ice. (Once again, why wasn't his nick-

---

[14] He also said Greenland had WMD's

49

name *Massive Liar*?) This is what we today call 'spin'. Some folks were duped, and with that Greenland was colonized, and has retained its silly name ever since. Contact was eventually lost through lack of shipping/lumber. The scandi settlements in Greenland were wiped out some time after 1400 with worsening climate.

Soon after Christianization, the Icelanders encountered the love of their millenium - writing! Oh how they loved to write! And sometimes read too! It was their heroin. In the period something like 1100-1300, the sagas were written. Later for that.

One day you may encounter some smug and trendy coffee shop patron (*101-Dwellers* we call them) who will tell you that us Icelanders have never fought a war or had armies - remember that thing about stamping on foot and poking the eye? Nuff said. There was an almost decent civil war in the 13th century, a period which was also the pinnacle of literature. Armies roamed the land, fighting each other, but they weren't particularly good at it. The bloodiest battle involved just over 100 deaths, and the most lethal weapons were rocks, thrown by hand. Really. It was a pretty disappointing affair all round, although economical. Iceland has a lot of rocks you see. People eventually got bored and signalled the King of Norway, hey, if you want to run this place, knock yourself out. We sure can't get the hang of it. That was the end of the old Republic and the entry into The Empire of Norway. No stormtroopers though. Still, this was a sizable empire, almost worth being part of. Besides Norway, it incorporated Iceland, Greenland, the Faeroes, Shetland, the Orkneys, Caithness, Sutherland, Ross, Dublin, Isle of Man, Anglesey, the Kola peninsula and chunks of Sweden. So... everything worthless in Northwest Europe. The King soon found he couldn't get no satisfaction, however. Transporting an army across the Atlantic in those days was just too damn risky, so he rented the land out for tax farming. *Smiður Andrésson* was an allegedly brutal Governor, who tried to squeeze the land for all its worth in terms of money, ladies and drink. *Grundar-Helga*, a Lady of the North, organized a party for him and his retinue, with wine and willing girls. In the night, surprise lulz, those guys got themselves massacred a bit. Apocryphal stories claim the guests were plied with drink and the girls turned their pant legs out so as to make it difficult to get them back on. While the guys were gettin' down an army gathered outside, and this party turned out pretty wild.

By the time people stopped fighting they had something else to occupy themselves with - staying alive. They weren't particularly good at that either. Cooling climate might be a bore in central Europe, but in Iceland it is a complete moodkiller, not to mention, a killer. When you don't have enough to eat, what could be an interesting addition to your life (or lack thereof)? Got it in one - plague! Smallpox; also Black Death; volcanic eruptions up to and including global implications. The Laki eruption alone wiped out 25% of the population and half the livestock and may even have put the French Revolution in motion. That should tell you it wasn't all whingeing. The population was reduced to a low of 20.000. They were so messed up that despite

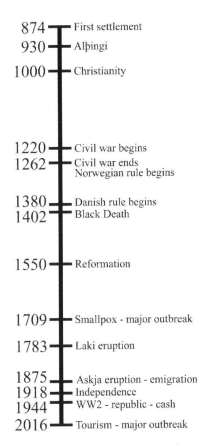

874 — First settlement
930 — Alþingi
1000 — Christianity

1220 — Civil war begins
1262 — Civil war ends
        Norwegian rule begins

1380 — Danish rule begins
1402 — Black Death

1550 — Reformation

1709 — Smallpox - major outbreak

1783 — Laki eruption

1875 — Askja eruption - emigration
1918 — Independence
1944 — WW2 - republic - cash
2016 — Tourism - major outbreak

the compulsion with writing everything down, people were too busy dying to properly jot down the names of Bishops in the 15th century. Even domesticated pigs went extinct. Must have sucked.

But the joke's on you, Norway! Meanwhile, the Black Death wiped out everybody who was anybody in Norway and the Danes inherited Iceland. Thank you very much fate! You think I'm being sarcastic now, don't you, but no. Let's face it - Danes aren't about much except drinking beer and looking at things. But as colonial masters - shop around if you like, but they are the best. They just about completely refrained from killing, just imposed some unjust trade, oh, and expropriated half the island through religious smoke and mirrors, which is the next episode.

You remember the Icelanders aren't all that serious about religion? They were catholics, not because they wanted to be, it just happened that way. The Icelandic priesthood never really warmed to the idea of celibacy - must have never got that memo. They all had, if not wives, then very serious girlfriends and lots of kids. That's how not serious they are. Even the Archbishop certified that Icelanders were hopeless romantics - as romantic as farm animals, that is to say. Anyway. It was 1550 and the King (of Denmark) now decided it was time for the Reformation. The Bishop of the South said *Whatever - LOL*, but the Bishop of the North said *Na-Ah!* as apparently the latter was the only one who had read the small print - with the reformation the church's possessions, which were now *yuge*, reverted to the King, who then owned half of all landed property in Iceland. The King had to send some muscle to cut his head off (and his two sons, you get the picture). Bish had yet a daughter though, and she encouraged revenge. A party of northern fishermen stationed around *Reykjanes* attacked the Governor's Deputy at *Kirkjuból*, killed him and all his company. Having gone to this trouble they thought, what they hey, and swept the entire peninsula, killing every single Dane they could lay their hands on.[15] (The lesson is - don't mess with the

---

[15] So far, the list of massacres of unwanted foreigners is starting to add up. This is not a hint to you, dear reader-tourist. Before researching my material I had only vague ideas of such events and did not set out to paint such a picture. Honest.

Ladies of the North.) Usually back in the day there was haunting in areas where violently killed people were hastily buried, and the Deputy's company was no exception. The locals knew how to deal with that though. They dug up the corpses, cut their heads off and reburied them with their noses rammed up their own bottom-cracks. That took care of that. This didn't go down too well in Denmark though, which must be ascribed to narrow-mindedness viz-a-viz cutting edge ghost removal techniques. Anyway, this was of no consequence. Not caring, the locals became Lutherans overnight - or overcentury. Who can tell. Finally, the clergy of this small island was able to enjoy the bliss of... whatever.

What good is having a colony if you don't earn anything from it? Iceland was a pretty miserable example, you could hardly even live there and expect to eat. But the King, as was the custom of the period, enforced a Royal Monopoly on all trade, selling licenses to profiteers during the 17th - 18th centuries. Make the suckers pay! There's not much more to say, except that Icelanders even to this day despise merchants and trade - in contrast to the English, just to name an example.

During the 17th century, Icelanders got wind of what was all the rage in Europe - burning people for witchcraft. There was some enthusiasm for this new project initially, but questionable results. In roughly 50 years only 170 prosecutions went forward, and they got around to burning no more than 20 men and one woman. Shortage of firewood may have been a factor. Even the last guy scheduled for burning got a royal pardon. Pretty weak stuff. As usual, the Icelanders wanted to do as everyone else, but just didn't get it. Apparently, the general idea was to burn women. But hey.

One has to mention something Icelanders were actually really incredibly serious about: Population control. Since they were now Christians they could no longer dispose of unwanted babies or throw the elders off cliffs. The land could only support a strictly limited number of people, and the thought of people of mixed genders inter-fering with each other and randomly adding to the total sent shivers down the spines of community leaders, because everyone had to be fed, and those who could not feed themselves had to be supported by the community. All the while the ghost of hunger was knocking at the door. So they came up with a set of simple rules:

1. If you had landed property (the best kind of property), you could get married and have kids.

1a. Ok, also if you were a tenant on a property, go for it.

2. If you did not have property you were not allowed to get married.

3. If you had sex outside marriage, you were executed.

3a. Usually the only proof of sex outside marriage was the birth of a child. If you were the mother, you were executed. The child was spared. The father was also spared, in prac-tice. If you want to relate that to misogyny, then do that, go forth and lead a happy life. Otherwise do bear in mind this was before the discovery of DNA. Put it together.

So, in practice, if you didn't have property, you had no future. You didn't really have a life. People bandy this phrase about a lot, but this IS not having a life. Things are much better now. You can be a complete waster and still enjoy the best life has to offer, such as lounging in a downtown coffee shop.

The 19th century saw the population of Iceland again reach the 60.000 mark. Phew!

Then came a long and really boring struggle for independence. Hint: the guy on the 500 kr note. That's all I feel like saying, and you should thank me.

Housing in Iceland evolved from the Viking/scandi longhouse, which had earthen walls and thatched roof, a main entrance and no windows to speak of. The scale of these buildings was somewhat grand.[16] With dwindling resources such as firewood and supporting timbers, this evolved to the Icelandic homestead, which consisted mostly of the thatched roof and sometimes a wood-panel facade. Often no walls were discernible. The scale of these structures was smaller than before, and the internal arrangement evolved toward the bathing quarters as the habitation module, serving as both living room and sleeping quarters for all. This was known down the centuries by its original name (*Baðstofa*) even though there was no bathing taking place there particularly - another thing Icelanders gave up on (the Vikings were known for cleanliness, but latter-day Icelanders were dirty). From outside it appeared as the inhabitants emerged out of the earth - so, there was invented the Hobbit hole.[17] Examples still exist, but keep in mind that those are generally late era high-end properties.[18] The Thatched Homestead (*Torfbær*) came to an end in the 20th century, even being banned in Reykjavík as unsanitary. It's worth mentioning that Icelanders never developed any native skill whatsoever in building out of stone. The Greenlanders did, however. Early 20th century building style was typically Scandinavian (though more austere) - wooden structure, multi-room apartments, sloping roof. Reykjavík West Side is a rich example. During WW2 the occupying armies built thousands of prefabricated, half-cylinder shaped dwellings (*Braggi*, pl. *Braggar*). After the war, the locals moved in. Never considered upmarket housing, some stigma attached to the new occupants. A few remain in use to this day. Post-war construction has emphasised concrete, and a lot of it. Thick walls, lots of reinforcing iron and a keen focus on thermal insulation. In a place of hostile weather AND earthquakes, not to mention a nuclear target high up the list during the Cold War, Icelanders have since built to withstand hell. (*Draw the blinds my*

---

[16]See the historical exhibit at *Stöng, Þjórsárdalur*.

[17]This (the author's own) hypothesis is entirely plausible. Tolkien borrowed a lot from Icelandic culture, see chapter 3.

[18]*Árbæjarsafn* museum

dear, I think I see the nuclear missile approaching.) I won't swear to it, but apparently the US military did adopt the Icelandic building style as their code.

In terms of economics, the main tradable commodity and export produced in Iceland historically was *Vaðmál*, a thick weave cloth of woolen thread. It was even a currency equivalent from very early on. As opposed to pounds of silver, trade occurred in yards of vaðmál, although eventual payment might be in different goods. This was the dominant export until early modern times, when fish products started pushing into first place. Early official seals representing Iceland carried a fish motif. Fish remains the top value export, with keen competition from aluminium and (you know it) tourism. Notable historical markets include Spain and Portugal[19] for salted fish (*Bacallao*), Nigeria for stockfish, and Britain during WW2 for fresh fish and other varieties. During the Battle of the Atlantic this was an important source of high protein food for the population of the UK. While the Greenland settlements survived, there was considerable trade in ivory through Iceland with the rest of Europe (and no, not from elephants) or so historians suggest. In recent history, Icelandic economics are mostly those of idiots. Since the start of independent monetary policy (1922), the *Króna* has devalued consistently and severely. Inflation was particularly rampant in the 70's and 80's when idiots even went so far as automating it through the job market. The Króna today is worth about 3% of what it was 35 years ago. The working man has traditionally paid for lax economic policy through the tools of inflation and devaluation, although unemployment since 1940 has been low to nonexistent. Recently, Iceland has followed the global trend for low inflation, a rather remarkable turn of events. The economy has traditionally been lacking in diversity, this is especially true of exports. Since Iceland needs to import a lot of stuff such as fuel, machinery and foods, the economy is highly

---

[19]They are the thugs who forced us into early repeal of prohibition of wine: *You no drink de wine, we no buy de bacalao!*

export-driven. Fisheries entrepreneurs used to stand closest to God. Today they are often regarded as Enemies of the People. I can't explain why, and I've said too much already. Ask your friendly coffee drinker.

Toward the end of the 19th century, Icelanders may have had a reason to feel they were home free. They had endured 1000 years of hell and scraped through. New sciences and technologies promised to make life more feasible and profitable in an otherwise shitty corner of the world. But then our old friend, volcanism, stepped in. This time it was *Askja* that covered the land in geological phlegm. So what's new? What was new was that this time, people actually could say, *This isn't funny anymore, I'm leaving!* - and leave they did, by the thousand. Most ended up in central Canada (*Gimli, Manitoba*), where there's still a community that keeps the flame alive. It even has a *Reykjavik* and an astronaut. *West-Icelanders* they are called, like they never left. They just took up temporary residence on a particularly remote peninsula, to exploit the birds' eggs or something, and are broadly expected back in the autumn. Btw Icelanders in the New World have never been much for that melting pot crap.

By WW2 Iceland was technically and practically independent. Almost. The Danes had left. There wasn't even any need to blow them up or shoot them, such as the Irish felt they needed to do with their colonial masters around the same time. Iceland was a separate kingdom yet still ruled by the King of Denmark. This is called a "Personal Union", rather than "Unwelcome Attention". Then the Germans invaded Denmark and the King was grounded. Then the British invaded Iceland. Then the Americans took over from the British (even before the US entered WW2, if you want to know - they pretty much stayed until 2005). Now, you might think that this would be a good time for us, the Icelanders, to give the old King, the Finger, what with three major armies standing between us. And you'd be right. It was an incredibly good time for such a gesture. If you are not the King of Denmark, that is. Or The Man in the Street

57

in Denmark, just going through 5 years of humiliating occupation, to be further humiliated by those people you had come to regard as your quaint yet lovable pets. All this time you'd thought they were so happy and grateful for the fatherly embrace of good ol' Denmark, to suddenly find out they'd rather kiss a Skunk Bird. Must have felt pretty cold. But that was that. Iceland became a completely independent Republic again - overlooking the now complete dependence on the United States. Sucks to you, Denmark! But thanks for giving the Skins back - and everything. If it had been the English as colonial masters we'd have really got to know what sucking is, probably would've had to pay them to GTFO in the end - and the Skins would still be in the British Museum.

But all of that aside, what you need to understand about this whole WW2 situation, is that it was a lovely war and that's an understatement. Icelanders referred to it as the *Blessed War*, if you want to know. Before 1940 Iceland was the poorest, biggest no-hoper loser country in Northwest Europe. Even Ireland was better, which takes some beating. Icelanders made so much money out of the British army during the war - yet nothing compared to what they made out of the American army - that at the end of it they were sitting on top of a pile of cold hard cash, mostly in dollars. They were golden. Nobody made as much cash out of the war as Icelanders did, proportionally speaking. Sweden? Switzerland? Amateurs. But since Iceland declared war on Germany in 1944, which soon led to the capitulation of Germany (maybe, you don't know!) they became eligible for Marshall Aid. Now, since they already made so much money war profiteering, it is only logical that they.... yes indeedy! - got proportionally bigger share of Marshall aid than any other country! So, your pockets are empty, your rent is due - and then you win the lottery, twice! But give them some credit, they actually spent the money on something sensible, state of the art fishing vessels, when they could have built a huge golden statue or something.

Oh all right, so it wasn't all song and dance, although there was a lot of that, mostly Swing. Iceland was an undeclared participant in WW2. Icelandic ships joined Allied convoys, and made the hazardous solo trip to Britain. This is where the good-natured Icelander shone through. In the convoy system there was a standing order that no freighter would stop to pick up survivors from a sunken one. This rule wasn't to the Icelanders' liking (being highly contrary to centuries-old tradition of survival on and by the sea), so they just ignored it, as is their way. This directly led to the greatest, and stupidest, maritime disaster of Icelandic history, the sinking of the *Goðafoss.*

WW2 not only made the Icelanders. It changed them. As you can imagine they were a bunch of dry, austere, timid creatures, always worrying about spending too much, or even anything - except on Brennivín. Their penchant for ludicrous excess? That started after WW2, but did not properly break out until the 90's. They were actually sort of communists[20] from 1945 until embracing Reaganomics. Only since then have they been able to properly express their lovable but crazy selves. That's not an endorsement btw.

The postwar years brought a string of conflicts known as *The Cod Wars.*[21] They were each triggered when Iceland unilaterally expanded an economic exclusion zone, a novelty at the time, eventually to 200 nmi. This was contested by various European countries with fishing interests, but effectively only by the British Navy and fishing fleet. What we are talking about here is perhaps the height of lunacy: Four tiny patrol vessels armed with 19th century artillery going against one of the premier naval powers of the world. Fortunately, the wars were fought by means of ramming and cutting of trawl cables, as opposed to a turkey shoot. It is perhaps worth dwelling on, and an insight into the national character, that although

---

[20]Don't believe me? You already know about the beer. Get this: apart from the government (2 radio channels and 1 TV) broadcasting was illegal until 1986; there was no TV on thursdays and likewise for the entire month of July.

[21]Not to be confused with the *Fish Slapping Dance*

at least the last two cod wars were predictable and entirely of Iceland's making, the Icelandic government made very little preparation to ensure that its coast guard could prevail in a ramming contest. A single fatality is recorded. Many ships were damaged, including at least one British frigate effectively destroyed. Iceland threatened to quit NATO and close the Keflavík base (an important US/NATO air base during the Cold War), and even considered procuring ships from the Soviet Union. In a strange echo of the Battle of New Orleans, AFTER the final cod war had been settled, a confrontation resulted in a serious ramming by a British warship. The Icelandic captain ordered the crew to man the guns, but no further action ensued. All three cod wars concluded in Iceland's favor, guaranteeing Icelandic control over local fishing - a hugely important economic goal, and just in time too. Today, fishing in this zone is generally sustainable and profitable, while most other fish stocks in European waters have been destroyed. If you wonder why Iceland never joined the EU... stop wondering.

Iceland has no railroads, you may notice. When at last the building of a rail line might have made economic sense, the automobile was already king. That's a good thing btw, trains are boring and not really that economical or environmentally friendly. Since we are on the subject, Iceland is a car-friendly country. Icelanders like their cars many, big, and with 4-wheel drive. Discounting countries under 40,000 population (who do they think they are, anyway?), Iceland ranks second worldwide in road motor vehicle ownership. Electric cars have started to appear, but they suffer in cold weather.

The *Ringroad* (Hringvegurinn, route 1) was only completed in 1974 - so you could say it took 1100 years to build. The last bit was crossing the rivers in the southeast. Glacial waters are bad enough, but since *Vatnajökull* covers some very active volcanoes, this area gets flash floods every few years which sweep the bridges away. The Department of Roads stand by with materials and usually have the bridges rebuilt in a couple of days(!)

Icelanders are the world's top consumers of electricity, per-capita, even though they don't use it for heating. It's one of a trove of per-capita world records they hold. The bulk ($\sim$80%) is consumed by the aluminium industry. Icelandic energy is mostly clean. The second half of the 20th century saw great strides in the harnessing of hydropower, capped with the *Kárahnjúkar* dam of 2009. You don't get much cleaner than that. However, more recently the emphasis has been on geothermal-electric power stations, such as at *Hellisheiði*. Superheated steam is used to power turbines. While it may not be as dirty as a tourist's underwear, it is pretty whiffy, releasing both CO_2 and noxious H_2S. The moss is not amused. The renewability of such installations is also suspect. On the other hand, straight geothermal installations are perhaps the most important energy asset in Iceland, utilized now for some 90 years. Hot water ($<100°$C) is pumped out of the ground and used for heating. Very cheap (people leave their windows open in winter) and efficient, the lower extraction temperature ensures negligible pollution as well. Wind power is in a probationary stage, but could very well be a strong addition. Reason: The hydropower output is at a minimum in February-ish, and that's when winds are at a maximum. However, think about this while you are out in the stillness of nature: how much would you not want to have the hum of wind turbines in the background? This project could run into performance issues if not carefully handled, because Icelanders love the outdoors and have a lot of rifles.

Reforestation is an ongoing effort since the mid-20th century. The aboriginal forest was Birch, which mostly disappeared through the centuries of human and ovine habitation - a major environmental catastrophe, and an ongoing one, in that sheep farming prevents recovery - the equivalent of an Original Sin in the mind of the informed Icelander.[22] Birch doesn't stand up well to the depredations of people and sheep, and never produced good timber anyway. Therefore,

---

[22]I did my National Service (as I choose to think of it) at the Government Forestry - did two tours

reforestation focuses on imported evergreens, in particular order, Pine, Fir, Larch, and other types. Pine has thrived, Fir has done mostly OK, but Larch has been problematic, prone to disease. Recently, the first ever harvest of lumber was produced in Iceland, and as a building material, Icelandic lumber is the best in the world. Yes it is. It's because the trees grow so slowly here, mkay. Only a slight embarrassment that this first harvest was utilized as firewood at a smelting plant. Pretend I never told you that. Loss of topsoil is a major problem, leaving swathes of land as near-desert. A gambit on that theme was the introduction of Alaskan Lupin. It's a hardy, arctic plant, unusual in that it gets nitrogen from the air and therefore needs no soil; rather it binds nitrogen in its root system, actually generating nutritious soil. The downside for the plant (but an upside for everyone else) is that its nitrogen-capturing system is energy intensive, so the Lupin can't face any competition for sunlight. Therefore, the first plant to take advantage of the generated soil will kill the surrounding Lupins by casting a shadow. The Lupins disappear, leaving the land transformed. This process takes some decades, however - entirely too long a time for the Icelandic temperament (they want everything yesterday). The Lupin has been declared an invasive species - and it's true, they are everywhere now, bluer than blue - and efforts have been mounted to clear them out of designated areas. These efforts have been expensive and mostly futile, as the Lupin is very hardy indeed. Sometimes such a program has succeeded in destroying all plant life in a given area EXCEPT the Lupin, go figure. It seems they are here to stay until they destroy themselves - fortunately, this is already happening in some areas. What is called for in the meantime, is Lupins of different colors.

In 1970 Iceland was internationally recognized by *Led Zeppelin*. A concert was given at the university in Reykjavík. It was the first time someone cool (apart from *Winston Churchill*) had been to Iceland. *Robert Plant* was moved to write a song to commemorate the occasion. No points for guessing which song.

3. The Language of Idiots

This chapter is devoted to helping you, the reader-tourist, to avoid embarrassment when pronouncing the name of the volcano that has just grounded your flight and ruined your holiday, and help you when reading road signs and maps. There's also some useless (even for Trivial Pursuit) information on literature - if you don't want that, skip a couple of pages. As always, this chapter will stay completely factual, if factitious. Btw, knowledge of this chapter is essential if you have hopes of winning *Tourist of the Month*.

The Icelandic language is in fact the original Scandinavian language spoken with little variation throughout Norway, Denmark, Sweden and Iceland in the period ca. AD 500-1300. After that the other Scandophones started diverging but Icelanders stuck with it. Especially during the reformation the other scandi languages got corrupted. Reason: they couldn't be bothered to make their own Bible translations so they had to make do with German Bibles. Icelanders and anything to do with putting pen to paper - you know it, the New Testament was already translated 10 years before the Reformation was completed, and the rest followed.

Literature

Old Icelandic literature is very much that, Icelandic, even though the language involved was at the time of creation shared by several much larger nations. The other Scandis did a little bit of writing and poetry, but really, actually, here

A Skin

were to be found the Chuck Norrises of literature in those days. There is strong evidence that the overwhelming majority of sagas, fiction as well as nonfiction, was written in Iceland. The biggest hint? Most of the stories mostly happen in Iceland. Even the biographies of the Kings of Norway, Denmark and Sweden (most or all) were written by Icelandic chroniclers. What we know of norse mythology comes especially from the works of the champion of champions of writing, Snorri Sturluson (13th c.), a poet, author of chronicles, nonfiction and historical fiction sagas. Also a warlord and major participant in the civil war - but a MUCH better writer than warlord (he used to run away or hide under the bed).

What are these sagas that you hear so much about? Well... it's mostly prose fiction but usually based on true events, apparently, interspersed with genealogy and poetry. Very roughly, this was the invention the novel. Cervantes...? A wannabe. The fictional sagas usually deal with the duty of revenge in a semi-anarchic, pagan society. In subject matter and ethos they are most closely related/comparable to the westerns of American cinema - no joke! A man's gotta do what a man's gotta do? We had that 800 years before John Wayne put on a hat. The domesticated tourist may ask, what's this thing about revenge? Why is it so big and what's it good for? Well, in a world without police, neighborhood watch or gender studies, your only effective protection against a potential enemy - and in a society like that everyone is a potential enemy - is the certainty that if you are killed then your kinsmen will avenge your death. It is your lease of life. So, if in such a case you are a man to whom the duty of revenge falls for a murdered relative, and you shirk that duty, you have effectively abandoned your whole clan to the wolves. You better believe they'll think less than nothing of you.

Since there was so very little to talk about for such a very long time, the language has barely changed since the sagas were written. Any native speaker can read the sagas without any formal training, although the going is slow at first. True fact this.

The civil war period (1220-1262) gave rise to a raft of contemporary nonfictional, often firsthand accounts of events of the era, compiled in the volume *Sturlunga Saga*. The contrast with the classical sagas is striking, if not disturbing. The fictional sagas emphasize heroism, duty and achievement. Very little of that is to be found in Sturlunga, instead there's wanton cruelty, cold-blooded murder, mutilation, mass executions, cowardice, betrayal and neglect, and decidedly second-rate heroes.

Even poetry appears to have been monopolised. The courtly poets favored at the scandi royal courts were almost exclusively Icelandic. There is strong evidence to suggest that the arguably pinnacle works of poetry of the era (*Völuspá* - a description of events leading to Ragnarök, the end of the world; and *Hávamál* - a set of worldly advice for survival and well-being) were composed in Iceland, later written down. To name one such instance, the author of *Völuspá* clearly did not know what mistletoe is. It is a parasitic plant not found in Iceland, but which IS found in mainland Scandinavia.

Let's take a look at the closing verse of *Völuspá*. Unlike prose, this is tricky for moderners, even natives, to understand. Not only is the language archaic, the frequent allusions and highly confusing word order make things difficult, Yoda himself would have trouble. Even entire lines of a verse are out of order. The gist of the poem as a whole is that it is supposedly uttered by an evil soothsayer-witch (Völva) whom the gods (Æsir) have captured, roughly treated resulting in death, (she took a lot of killing, actually) and brought back to life with magic. They compel her to tell all she knows, which is the future doom of the race of Æsir and the end of the world (Ragnarök). The Völva tells this story at great length and in detail, all the while taunting the Æsir. Each of the leading Æsir reportedly meets his demise in battle with one of a host of long-dreaded monsters, who are finally let loose at the onset of Ragnarök. The final verse is a vision, a snapshot occurring during Ragnarök serving as a terrifying illustration. The spelling here is modern, Icelandic on the left, and English translation line by line on the right. The true meaning is not 100% certain even to experts; it's educated guesswork.

Þar kemur hinn dimmi	There comes the dark
dreki fljúgandi,	dragon, flying,
naður fránn neðan	serpent all-seeing, down
frá Niðafjöllum;	from Niða-mountains;
ber sér í fjöðrum,	carries in its feathers,
flýgur völl yfir,	flies across the fields
Níðhöggur nái.	Níðhöggur corpses,
Nú mun hún sökkvast.	now she sinks.

The dark dragon is named Níðhöggur. He flies hither from the Niða mountains, presumably his lair. He is of a race of serpents, and he sees everything. He carries the corpses of dead men stuck in his feathers, while he flies overhead. The last line is mysterious, but is interpreted as the Völva has now told all and is about to sink back into the darkness of hell, whence she was summoned by the magic of the Æsir.

Who are the Æsir? A family clan of imperfect personalities, the best of which is *Þór*, the god of thunder and the splitting of skulls with a hammer (also of driving, funnily enough - consider making a sacrifice to him before getting behind the wheel of your rental). *Þór* spends his time touring the badlands in his turbocharged billy-cart, doing burnouts and bashing the half-trolls who live there. Modern youth still look up to him. The top guy is *Óðinn*, who is as wise as a library soaked in LSD (he actually gave an eye for that), and there's the Defence Minister, *Týr*, who gave up his arm to trick a monstrous wolf into accepting a leash. Also *Freyr*, who is responsible for fertility and good lovin'. These four guys gave us the names of four days of the week[23] Then there are two fellas, suspected late additions to the pantheon under Christian influence - *Baldur*, the White, incredibly nice guy all round and do-gooder (Jesus?), and

---

[23] If you don't already know, try to figure it out - only this is lost to Icelandic. This happened as an example of religio-cultural self-harm during an off-season of the Unicelandic Committee. We got *Third-*, *Middle-*, *Fifth-* and *Fasting* days instead. How bland can you get?

Loki, a slippery character who is all too fond of trolling the other gods and getting them into trouble (The Devil?). *Loki* ends up getting *Baldur* killed in a permanent way through a devious scheme involving mistletoe. That time the other gods no longer just threaten *Loki* or slap him around, they finally go medieval on his ass. There are ladies too, of course. *Frigg* was *Óðinn's* wife, her specialty - wisdom and foreknowledge, whaddaya know... you'd have to get up pretty early in the morning to get anything past those two. Then there's *Freyja*, *Freyr's* sister, and she is the actual love goddess, and that of sex and fertility as well as gold and whatnot. In other words, HOT! She is married to a minor character, *Óður* (not to be confused with *Óðinn*), who must have got something going for him because *Freyja's* animal lust for him is attested.

Scenes from Ragnarök; the gods fight their final battle; the world burns.

Óður (the name means *Mad* or *Madman*) spends little time at home but makes long trips to wherever (this is NOT a ripoff of the Kardashians btw), leaving *Freyja* behind to suffer her need, crying tears of solid gold (THAT's bling). Then she goes out too, searching for *Óður* far and wide among many strange peoples. Are we thinking the same thing, that we're dealing with one seriously mad cat here? Final mention goes to *Sif*, *Þór's* wife, an earth goddess. People like to suggest she's been around the neighborhood - she does have a son of an unknown father. Indeed, those who sow the seed in the earth and reap the harvest, are many.

Further from *Völuspá*, a listing of Dwarves' names:

Þar var Mótsognir
mæstur um orðinn
dverga allra,
en Durinn annar;
þeir mannlíkun
mörg um gerðu
dvergar úr jörðu,
sem Durinn sagði.

Veigur og Gandálfur,
Vindálfur, Þráinn,
Þekkur og Þorinn,
Þrár, Vitur og Litur,
Nár og Nýráður,
nú hefi eg dverga,
- Reginn og Ráðsviður, -
rétt um talda.

Nýi og Niði,
Norðri og Suðri,
Austri og Vestri,
Alþjófur, Dvalinn,
Bívör, Bávör,
Bömbur, Nóri,
Án og Ánar,
Ái, Mjöðvitnir.

Fíli, Kíli,
Fundinn, Náli,
Hefti, Víli,
Hannar, Svíur,
Frár, Hornbori,
Frægur og Lóni,
Aurvangur, Jari,
Eikinskjaldi.

No translation necessary. Is there anything there at all familiar? Can you say: "Cultural appropriation"? No matter, there's plenty left. 10 points btw if you can identify that very last name.

The poem *Völuspá* is a major source on the ancient mythology that accompanied the pagan religion. A great many activities of the Æsir gods were aimed at staving off Ragnarök, their destiny - vainly on the face of it, as fate was considered immutable.

Historically, there have been claims, mostly by Norwegians, that this body of literature is Pan-Scandinavian rather than Icelandic. It is a claim that can either be regarded as meaningless (i.e. making no addition or modification to accepted knowledge), or as being with-

68

out foundation or evidence. Meanwhile, there is plenty of evidence to the contrary.

Further reading suggested (all available in translation):

• *Edda*, by *Snorri Sturluson*. If you are into mythology and stuff like that, you won't find a more interesting read. This gives you pretty much the works on the *Æsir*.

• *Völuspá*, unknown author. Nuff said.

• *Hávamál*, unknown author. Intriguing advice for an uncertain world. Topics include how to avoid being surprised by enemies, how to handle drink, how not to piss off your host (or any other thug), to not be a party-pooper, how to treat friends, to be brave, how to relate to women (trigger warning) and just to be plain smart! Could be useful after [insert favorite disaster motif here] destroys civilization - or if you get locked up in maximum security prison and need to ingratiate yourself with the Aryan mob as their high priest!

• *Egils Saga*, probably by *Snorri Sturluson*. If you want to get behind the wheel of the actual sagas, this is not the Rolls Royce (boring car anyway) but the sporty Mercedes; fluidly written. *Egill Skallagrímsson* was a viking, poet and adventurer of complex character, as outrageous as it was deep. Read about the skyr and beer binge on the White Sea! Also lots of killings, poetry and imagination. And imaginative killings. And poetry in lieu of killings. I could go on.

• *Völsunga Saga*, author unknown. One of the class of "ancient" sagas, already centuries old when written down. An heroic epic, possibly loosely based on historical events in or around 5th century Europe (appearance by *Attila the Hun*). Gives rise to speculation that the scandis were tearassing around Europe and the Roman Empire before settling in Scandinavia. You know *Wagner* opera, *Sigfried*, the *Nibelungs* and that? This story is where that material comes from. Also strikingly shares elements (sword stuck in a slab, couple illicitly sharing a bed, separated by a sword) with the legend of *King Arthur*, also rooted in the 5th century.

Folklore

Icelanders gave up on the Skins soon after the end of the Republic. Worsening climate and economic situation meant that there were no resources to create large books - they were fudging expensive. The original Skins were still floating around though, on the homesteads, so there was lots of reading going on even if there was precious little writing. It can hardly be a coincidence that Iceland enjoyed perhaps the highest literacy rate in the world up until modern times. But anyway. To replace writing, oral folklore developed, pretty similar to that of other European peoples. This folklore is made up of distinct short stories, recited in the long winter evenings (and they were long indeed). They were collected and printed in the 19th century, on the *Grimm Brothers* model. Notably, the stories are mostly free of gory horror, unlike for example German folklore as exemplified by the Grimm collection (pretty sick stuff, yeah, and I'm not even talking about the Disney versions). The stories are roughly classified in the genres of (some notable examples given):

• **Ghosts** - *The Deacon of Myrká*. The drowned deacon returns from the grave to claim his betrothed - unbeknownst to her, he is no longer among the living.

• **Trolls** - *The Santas family*. Grýla and Leppalúði are trolls and proud parents of the nine, some say thirteen, *jólasveinar*, or santas. Think *The Addams Family* on crack. Grýla is the brains of the operation. She goes around the countryside, collecting naughty kids which she brings home to the cave in a sack and cooks and eats them. Leppalúði (literally: *Rags-dork*) is a useless loafer. They have a monster cat, the Yule Cat. If you don't get any article of clothing for a Christmas present, the Yule Cat gets you (or steals your dinner anyway). The santas visit homesteads around Christmas time and they are not entirely a welcome bunch. A shower of bastards if there ever was one. See chapter 1.

- **Water-dwellers** - *Nykur* is a creature identical to a horse, except with back-turned hooves. If anybody mounts it, the Nykur charges into the water and drowns that person. A good example and far from unique, of a tale apparently calculated to scare children away from dangerous activities (mounting a strange horse).

- **Witchcraft** - *Galdra-Loftur* (Magic-Loftur) was an 18th century intellectual given to sorcery. Stories about his supposed exploits developed and are the subject of an eponymous modern stage play.

- **Saints and holymen** - *Sæmundur* the Learned was a historical figure (11th/12th c.), a clergyman educated abroad, allegedly in Paris. Many stories exist of his dealings with the *Devil*, in which the latter invariably gets the short end of the stick, outsmarted by *Sæmi*. Later popularised in lyrics and music by *Megas*.

- **Outlaws** - *Fjalla-Eyvindur* (Mountain-Eyvindur) was an 18th century individual who, along with his wife *Halla*, chose the outlaw life, living in the wilderness and rustling sheep. Documents show them appearing in different parts of the country. Many stories developed about their supposed exploits.

- **Fictional adventures** - *Búkolla*, the speaking, magical cow has several stories. In one she is rustled by a troll, but then rescued by the farmer's son. Búkolla helps engineer their escape through the magical powers of the hairs on her tail.

- **Comedies** - *Bakkabræður* (The Bakki Brothers). Typical idiots motif, Gísli, Eirkíkur and Helgi are three idiot brothers who appear in many stories, detailing their enormous stupidity. The humor might not tickle the nerve of the metropolitan tourist. *The Three Stooges* might compare.

- **Elves** • **Natural phenomena** • **Events** • **Superstitions**

Grammar

Icelandic - the language - is a highly inflected germanic language. Are you a non-native speaker of German? Find it hard? Icelandic is about 17 times harder, although quite similarly structured. The difference is mainly the degree of inflection. There are four cases as in German, but they are MUCH more active. Some nouns have the full four distinct cases, most have more than two. The cases are different for singular/plural, also the definite article is attached rather than freestanding and IS affected by the inflection. The indefinite article is nonexistent. How many different ways can YOU say "Horse"?

A Horse	The Horse	Horses	The Horses
Hestur	Hesturinn	Hestar	Hestarnir
Hest	Hestinn	Hesta	Hestana
Hesti	Hestinum	Hestum	Hestunum
Hests	Hestsins	Hesta	Hestanna

Confused yet? This is not *The Nine Billion Names of God*, but we're getting there. Now, adjectives inflect by gender, also affected by singular/plural AND article, AND comparative/ superlative, and get this: on top of the aforementioned, adjectives also have cases like nouns! Let's look at just the one adjective, *Svangur (Hungry)*. Take a deep breath before looking at the next page, and yes, the following is ALL in use in everyday speech, we're not like the French who save the really good stuff for writing only. The cases (as for nouns) are arranged vertically by fours, as for nouns above. They are repeated vertically through the 9 forms of gender and comparison. This comes to a grand total of 144 forms of inflection (English would have 3). Admittedly not all are distinct and some adjectives are simpler than this one.

	Hungry A, sing.	Hungry The, sing.	Hungry plural	Hungry The, pl.
(masculine)	svangur	svangi	svangir	svöngu
	svangan	svanga	svanga	svöngu
	svöngum	svanga	svöngum	svöngu
	svangs	svanga	svangra	svöngu
(masculine)	svengri	svengri	svengri	svengri
(comparative)	svengri	svengri	svengri	svengri
	svengri	svengri	svengri	svengri
	svengri	svengri	svengri	svengri
(masculine)	svengstur	svengsti	svengstir	svengstu
(superlative)	svengstan	svengsta	svengsta	svengstu
	svengstum	svengsta	svengstum	svengstu
	svengsts	svengsta	svengstra	svengstu
(feminine)	svöng	svanga	svangar	svöngu
	svanga	svöngu	svangar	svöngu
	svangri	svöngu	svöngum	svöngu
	svangrar	svöngu	svangra	svöngu
(feminine)	svengri	svengri	svengri	svengri
(comparative)	svengri	svengri	svengri	svengri
	svengri	svengri	svengri	svengri
	svengri	svengri	svengri	svengri
(feminine)	svengst	svengsta	svengstar	svengstu
(superlative)	svengsta	svengstu	svengstar	svengstu
	svengstri	svengstu	svengstum	svengstu
	svengstrar	svengstu	svengstra	svengstu
(neuter)	svangt	svanga	svöng	svöngu
	svangt	svanga	svöng	svöngu
	svöngu	svanga	svöngum	svöngu
	svangs	svanga	svangra	svöngu
(neuter)	svengra	svengra	svengri	svengri
(comparative)	svengra	svengra	svengri	svengri
	svengra	svengra	svengri	svengri
	svengra	svengra	svengri	svengri
(neuter)	svengst	svengsta	svengst	svengstu
(superlative)	svengst	svengsta	svengst	svengstu
	svengstu	svengsta	svengstum	svengstu
	svengsts	svengsta	svengstra	svengstu

You're probably feeling hungry by now. After this, verb conjugation seems pedestrian:

Fara	To Go	Hylja	To Cover
Fór	I Went	Huldi	I Covered
Fórum	We Went	Huldum	We Covered
Farið	We've Gone	Hulið	We've Covered

Icelandic language has been described by a resident Japanese priest as an instrument of oppression. I guess when it comes to oppression, the Japanese do know their stuff. A friendly suggestion: take up learning Icelandic! A friendlier suggestion: take up ramming skewers through your forearms!

Icelandic, like German, but as opposed to English, likes to link words into an unattractive mess. English would have the place name "Bridge River Falls" whereas Icelandic would have "Brúarárfoss". This does make your life somewhat harder, tourist, and there's not a lot of help to be offered there.

Pronounciation

Icelandic arguably has no dialects. There are some slight regional idiosyncrasies to pronounciation and word use, but even these are disappearing.

AÁBCDĐEÉFGHIÍJKLMN OÓPQRSTUÚVWXYÝZÞÆÖ

Special vowels

Á á : The vowel in "how"   **É é** : As "ye"   **Í í** : As "ee"

Ó ó : The vowel in "moan"   **U u** : Identical to Swedish **U u**

Ú ú : As "oo"   **Ý ý** : Same as **Í í**   **Æ æ** : The "i" in "mine"

Ö ö : The "u" in "urge"   **AU au** : As "oeil" (french)

EI ei : The vowel in "main" or "hay"

EY ey : Same as **EI** ei   Ø ø : That's danish!

Special consonants

The following two letters lead to perhaps the most head scratching among foreigners:

Ð ð : The "th" in "the" : never as initial of a word.

Þ þ : The "th" in "thing" : only as initial of a word.

One looks like a drunk and dishevelled **d** (the *Eth*), and the other like a surprised **p** (the *Thorn*). They are ridiculous. Why the heck did Icelanders invent them? They didn't. They got them from English, would you believe, with their original alphabet. With the introduction of printing in England (the typeset was German) those two nonstandard letters disappeared. Icelanders were never that big on printing, so they stuck with them.

LL ll : Oh dear, this is the big one! Guaranteed, when a major volcanic eruption occurs, this concoction crops up and ruins your day. Well, it's not simple (duh!). The sound is a combination of D and L, but a close one. The D and L don't form as completely distinct. The tongue position for forming the D sound is not behind your front teeth, but rather side touch to the inside of your cheek. The muffled D sound gives way immediately to an L splash. It helps to be just out of the dentist's office with anaesthesia and lots of drool. But be warned: words of foreign origin retain the standard L preceded by a short vowel, such as "halló". Be even more warned: There exists a slang shortening of the word "hallærislegur" (literal meaning: "having the air/appearance/feel as if affected by a poor agricultural year or harvest"; actual meaning: "he sucks"; mostly used by girls to describe inferior menfolk) and this short form is "halló" and DOES have the D-L splash pronounciation. Told you it wasn't simple.

G g : Okay, sometimes you have the standard hard G sound, and certainly so in words of foreign origin. Sometimes you have a soft, drawn out G sound which is hard to describe, imagine making a sound like a snake hissing, only much softer. If there's a rule involved, I've never heard of it, excepting that at the beginning of a word there is always a hard G. I'm sure there is a rule. There's definitely a rule. There's always a rule for stuff like this, but I don't want to know what it is, and neither do you!

FN fn : as "bn", unless someone is trying too hard to be clear-spoken or just has a broomstick up his bottom, then simply as "fn".

FL fl : likewise as "bl".

C c, Q q, W w, Z z : Never used. Unicelandic. What is the point of them anyway?

All together now!

Eyjafjallajökull = AIYAFYADLAYUKUDL

and don't forget the D-L splash (underlined). Note that all vowels in this word are long, except the second "a" and the "u". A lot of why this is so hard is your own fault, English speakers. Your pronounciation is pretty messed up too.

Traditional Music

Now, Icelanders may have been all about books, but they weren't about much when it came to music back in the day. There was only one kind of traditional instrument (*Langspil*), and that had only two strings. Ok, so I exaggerate (or downplay?). Anyway, there were a couple of folk songs and catchy later compositions, such as:

• *Móðir mín í Kví Kví* (Traditional) - The tune to this is sad enough, but if you want to really get into the vein of sadness that was being an Icelander, then study those lyrics and what they mean. I can't help, it's too much for me. The author/publisher assume no responsibility for any insanity or suicide.

• *Krummavísur* (19th c.) - Dedicated to Iceland's coolest bird, the

Raven, and his struggles and exploits.

• *Ólafur Liljurós* (Trad.) - A so-called *Vikivaki* (not *Wikiwiki*), a dance poem. *Ólafur* is tempted by the pagan elven maidens to join with them. Is his conviction strong, or will his integrity be compromised by elven sluts? Btw the dance tradition was mostly stamped out by the church as a source of immorality, notably surviving in the Faeroes.

• *Sá ég spóa* (Trad.) - A mindless song about birds. Capable of extreme levels of annoyance as canon performance.

• *Á Sprengisandi* (20th c.) - The rider crossing the sands north of *Vatnajökull* has a lot on his mind - or is his mind playing tricks on him? What worldly or supernatural creatures may lie in wait or be secretly shadowing him, with homicidal intent? Will his horse make it through and save the day?

• *Í Hlíðarendakoti ("Fyrr var oft í koti kátt")* (19th c.) - A popular feelgood song, perfect for camping.

• *Þingvallasöngur ("Öxar við ána")* (19th c.). Apart from actual independence, the best thing to come out of the struggle for independence. Very nationalistic, and unyielding; no room for compromise. This is the unofficial national anthem (I won't even mention the real one, it's that awful), the equivalent of *Waltzing Matilda* for Australia.

• *Brennið þið vitar* (20th c.) - The sailors pray for the lighthouses to burn through the dark and guide them home. This song inspired *The Trammps* to write the hit *Disco Inferno*.[24]

• *Sofðu unga ástin mín* (20th c./Trad.) - A lullaby.

[Youtube: "Idiots in Iceland - Traditional music playlist"]

---

[24] No, not really

Small Names

Icelanders usually have a first name, a middle name and a patronymic. A small percentage of families maintain a family last name of the internationally traditional kind. The origin of first and middle names is most frequently either original Scandinavian or from the Bible. The patronymic is almost always the father's name followed by *-son* for a male individual or *-dóttir* for a female individual. Recently, and more rarely, people carry a patronymic for the mother instead of the father, or even a patronymic for each parent.

Sometimes a son carries the same name as his father giving rise to a tautonym, *Jón Jónsson* etc. This never happened in olden days, e.g. you don't find this in the sagas, ever. The reason: giving a name to a child involved an implicit wish that the new individual would be like a certain older relative or other person carrying that name, and was therefore a strong compliment. A father who gave a son his own name would therefore be guilty of massive hubris to the point of ridicule. People were sensitive about such matters back then; somewhere down the ages they lost the plot.

Active family names usually stem from Danish or other scandi families, such as merchants, that established themselves in Iceland typically in the 19th century, e.g. *Schram, Proppé* etc. There are some that reference localities or areas in Iceland like *Breiðfjörð*, but sarcastic voices claim those names came about when mothers were unable to name a father of the child. Then there are always some simply invented by lunatics, such as *Gnarr* - NOT related to *Gnarrenburg*, Germany.

Not any name is recognized. A christian name must be an Icelandic name already in use, or a new name that is grammatically sensible and has some measure of Icelandic cultural provenance, and is not detrimental to wellbeing. Otherwise, the name is rejected by the

Unicelandic Committee[25] and is refused registration by the Registry Office. New surnames are generally not allowed. However, they don't go as far as arresting you for what you call yourself in public.

Xenophobia in so Many Words

Icelandic is the most xenophobic language on this planet - to best knowledge. It hates with a passion the idea of officially adopting foreign words. That is not to say it never happens effectively, even if unofficially. However, there's a longstanding and dynamic effort, not to say movement, to create and adopt new words of Icelandic origin for every new concept that otherwise would require adoption of a foreign word. This has been happening since the 19th century, even independently of the Unicelandic Committee. This is our way of making a difficult language even more inscrutable. Some examples:

• **Sími** - Telephone. An archaic word originally meaning *String* or *Cord* was brought back from the dead to represent this new invention. It even covers modern mobile phones, despite the fact that they are cordless. Near-universal usage, see below.

• **Gemsi** - Mobile phone. Original or recent meaning - *Troublemaker*. Sounds similar to the acronym *GSM*. Limited usage.

• **Tölva** - Computer. The ancient word *Völva*, meaning *Soothsayeress*, was given a makeover by changing the initial to *T*, which is also the initial for *Tala - Number*. Now, sarcasm may be preferred sometimes, but this is some pretty nifty piece of wordbuilding, it has to be admitted (For contrast, just look up what the Swedes came up with). Universal usage.

• **Þyrla** - Helicopter. A noun derived from a similar verb meaning *To Whirl*: - A *Whirler*. Universal usage.

• **Lögregla** - Police. A combination word, the first part means *Law*

---

[25]It actually exists - it's called *Mannanafnanefnd*

and the second part means (don't laugh) *Order*. So when in trouble, you call the *Laworder*. Could easily be a TV show. The short is *Lögga*. Universal usage.

- **Sjónvarp** - Television. Another combination, the first part means *Vision* and the second part means *Cast*. So during your stay you might watch the *Visioncast*. Universal usage.

- **Vél** - Machine. Archaic, originally meaning *trickery*, especially by witchcraft, to achieve a certain end. Somewhat echoes *Machination*. Universal usage.

- **Vafri** - Browser. A noun derived from a similar verb meaning *To Wander* (aimlessly). Common usage.

- **Rafmagn** - Electricity. This phenomenon was historically first observed via amber (*Raf*). The second part of the word means some kind of inherent natural or supernatural effect or conjuration. So - the *Conjuration of Amber*. Universal usage.

- **Skjár** - Monitor. Archaic word for *Window*. Then again, what usually is displayed on a monitor? Windows! Universal usage.

- **Ljósvaki** - Aether. This was a concept (now obsolete) in physics before the 20th century - a supposed form of matter that allowed light waves to propagate. A combination, the first part means *Light* and the second is a noun derived from the verb *To Wake*. So - *Lightwaker*. Still used by pretentious radio presenters as a self-description. Otherwise extinct.

The French Connection

Do you know what your own name means? This section does not regard Icelandic language as such, but rather how proto-germanic and Scandinavian names have survived, albeit corrupted, in foreign languages including especially French and English, and how they can be decoded through Icelandic. This may be interesting to the really anal reader-tourist.

There are mainly three historical connections that matter here:

1. The Franks were a germanic tribe who conquered Gaul from the 5th century onwards. They adopted a Latin language but retained many germanic names which in their uncorrupted form would be understandable to modern Icelandic speakers with a good secondary education, even though not all of these appear in Icelandic literature.

2. The Normans were a host of Vikings from Norway, Denmark and Iceland who conquered Normandy from c. 900 AD. They eventually adopted French language and likewise retained Scandinavian names. From 1066 they conquered England too.

Those classes of names largely still exist in French and other languages, especially English.

3. Scandinavian influence in Britain and Ireland (so nothing to do with the French then) in the period c. 800 - 1066 AD.

• **Robert** - Hróðbjartur. The meaning is *Fame + Bright* - the Bright Fame - who wouldn't want that? Think Kim Kardashian. Modern Icelandic has slightly corrupted this to *Hróbjartur*.

• **Richard** - Ríkharður. The meaning is *Powerful + Hard* - you don't get any tougher than that. *Rík-* comes from *Ríkur* as in *Rich*, but note that this word does NOT originally mean *wealthy*.

• **William** / **Guillaume** / **Liam** - Vilhjálmur. The meaning is *Will + Helmet* - taking that further is anybody's guess.

• **Tancred** - Þakkráður. The meaning is *Thanks + Advice* - the well thanked advice/advisor. Can't say fairer than that. This name does not appear in the sagas, is highly corrupted, so it's a good bet that it's Frankish rather than Norman.

• **Camembert** - this is the name of a village in Normandy as well as cheese. The meaning is unknown to this author, but comparing to *Robert* removes pretty much all doubt that it is germanic in origin, probably Norman.

• **Roland** / **Orlando** - <u>Hróðland</u> The meaning is *Famous + Land*. Older than the Norman conquests, not found in the sagas. Frankish.

• **Gilbert** - <u>Gíslbjartur</u> The meaning is *Hostage + Bright*, a bright hostage. Perhaps hostage keeping was a more mainstream activity in olden days. Frankish, as above.

• **Roger** - <u>Hróðgeir</u> The meaning is *Famous + Spear*.

• **Ronald** / **Reginald** - Rögnvaldur / Reginvaldur. The meaning of the first part *Rögn- / Regin-* is a little hazy, but is a kind of divine advice, decision and/or power. The latter part means *Ruler*, so, a ruler who is favored by or in the confidence of the gods. Wasn't that true of *Ronald Reagan*?

• **Adelaide** - <u>Aðalheiður</u>. The first part *Aðal-* means *Noble*. The second part can mean *Bright* or *Beauty* or *Honor* or all of those at the same time. Not half bad. So.... everything Australia isn't?

Quaint but Common Words and Phrases

Either import these unchanged into your own language or transliterate, if you want to sound clever.

1. **Drullaðu þér** - **Drulla** means *mud*. Best translation could be *mud off*, as in *get the hell out*. Rude, verging on insulting.

2. **(Litla) Rassgat** - Literally: *(Little) Asshole*. Term of endearment of infants only. You wouldn't call an adult this. It wouldn't register as an insult, it would just be ridiculous - although you can say **Farðu í rassgat**, same meaning as *Vaffanculo* - very rude.

3. **Jæja** - Soft exclamation, akin to *Well*, but more ubiquitous and with no independent meaning. Whenever an Icelander doesn't know what to say, this word is a strong candidate. See appendix A (Party pooper).

4. **Ha?** - Again, exclamation akin to *What?*, but more ubiquitous and with no independent meaning. Strong favorite if your wife is

nagging you while you're watching the game on TV.

5. **Éttu það sem úti frýs** - Literally: *Eat what freezes outside* (imperative) - presumably a carcass/carrion in winter. Similar in use to *Fuck off*. Definitely rude and can easily be taken as an insult. Try this on your tourist friends in winter.

6. **Eins og skrattinn úr sauðarleggnum** - Literally: *Like the devil out of the sheep's leg* - presumably when broken for the marrow. Describes something wholly unexpected, like *Donald Trump* winning the election.

7. **Gráir fyrir járnum** - Literally: *Grey with iron* (plural). A force very well armed and battle-ready (armed to the teeth).

8. **Nota sem Grýlu** - Literally: *Use as a Grýla*. Grýla is the mother of the santas, a terrifying she-troll. Describes politics of fear. Early example of trolling(?) *Project Fear* (Brexit) was a Grýla. Totally.

9. **Þar fór góður biti í hundskjaft** - Literally: *A good piece ended up in a dog's mouth*. A coveted prize fell to someone unworthy or inferior. Like *Kim Kardashian* marrying *Kanye West*.

10. **Varpað út í hafsauga** - Literally: *Thrown in the ocean's eye*. Something utterly and completely rejected or discarded. Like the EU may be sometime in the future.

11. **Ríður ekki feitum hesti frá þessu** - Literally: *(He/She) doesn't ride a fat horse from this*. A fat horse signifies a well fed and valuable animal. An enterprise has turned out badly for someone, resulting in loss of property, prestige etc. Think *Angela Merkel*.

12. **Drasl** - Literally: *Junk*. Slang puts this word on a par with *shit* in English: crude but inoffensive. Adopt this word for something annoying, questionable or outstanding: *This is just the drasl!*

13. **Hefur munninn fyrir neðan nefið** - Literally: - *has the mouth below the nose*. Yeah right. Someone who calls a spade a spade, hard-hitting expression, pulling no punches, and to the point.

Dirty Words

Let's lose all pretense now and cover the swear words. If you are a Metropolitan tourist of gentle nature, skip this section. These are mostly variations on the theme of the devil and hell or dirt and excrement. Sexual allusions are rare. OK, so Icelanders aren't the world champions of swearing. These do go up to 11.

1. **Helvítis** - Your generic angry outburst, (Damn!) or a qualifier for something to follow. Literally: something from hell.

2. **Djöfulsins** - Similar to 1, except to do with the devil.

3. **Andskotans/Andskotinn** - Same thing again, archaic euphemism for the devil, literally: The Enemy.

4. **Skíthæll** - Literally: Shit-heel. An evil bastard.

5. **Drullusokkur** - Literally: Mud-sock. Another baddie.

6. **Kúkalabbi** - Literally: Poo-walker. Someone who walks around in or with poo. This is more your pitiful loser jerk.

7. **Hálfviti** - Literally: Half-wit. Your basic putdown.[26]

8. **Bjáni** - Roughly: Idiot.

9. **Fífl** - Literally: Fool.

10. **Asni** - Literally: Ass (Donkey).

11. **Drusla** - Literally: Rag. Akin to Slut.

What have we learnt? Translate this: *Drullaðu þér, helvítis kúkalabbi!*

Let's go the other way too. Remember this? *...you damn dirty ape!*: ...helvítis skíta-apinn þinn!

You just don't get this from other guide books.

---

[26] A frequent misspelling of this word drops the (silent) f. That's when it blows back up in the user's face.

4. Dos, Don'ts and No-Nos

In this chapter we will examine some aspects of behaviour, etiquette and manners - what to do and what not to do. Some is for your benefit (saving you embarrassment), some is for ours (reducing Iceland's idiot-footprint), and some is a bit of both. (Remember when I said the locals still like you? "Still" is the key word here. Don't make it "used to".) These are the situations that can bring humiliation, resentment and hatred. Also tar and feathers. Maybe.

Major financial considerations and situations potentially resulting in death or serious injury will be covered later.

DON'T tip.

Reasons: (We'll take the whole Reservoir Dogs thing as read - including the chair and razor).

1. Icelanders don't - isn't that reason enough?

2. Tipping is stupid.

3. You don't feed the zoo animals.

4. Tipping is a form of emotional blackmail, hence reasons 1 and 2.

5. The service industry workers here are paid plenty enough (unless it's a shady operation, in which case you shouldn't do business there at all), there's no reason to tip them.

6. If you do tip, and let's face it there's about 2 million of you and only 300.000 of us, tipping is eventually going to become accepted in this country, and depress the fixed wages of

the workers. We don't want that so BUTT OUT!

7. Tipping is not expected of you here.

8. Save your money.

DON'T toss coins into any old body of water when in *Þingvellir*.

Reasons: Okay, there's a long tradition of tossing coins into ONE particular crevice at Þingvellir nicknamed *Peningagjá*, real name *Flosagjá*. Since tourists started to arrive in humongous numbers they've got it into their heads that we can't approach a clear puddle without emptying our pockets. That's not how it works people! Let's also bear in mind that to us, *Þingvellir* is a holy place, the birthplace of the nation and symbol of unity since 930 AD combined with unique natural beauty. Think of the Liberty Bell dangling from Stonehenge, perched above Niagara Falls. Now, when you walk the paths of *Þingvellir* and every single stream and pool has coins in it, it looks ridiculous and spoils the mood, not least when taking into account that one of those is a historical place/means of execution. You don't enter a gothic cathedral and distribute coins all over the floor do you?

DO toss coins into the original *Flosagjá* at Þingvellir.

Reasons: It's tradition, and it is allowed. Also, coins at the bottom of this particular crevice look really cool. Don't throw your credit cards in though.

Off-road driving is a **NO-NO.**

Reasons:

1. It is very illegal.

2. It carries a heavy fine, typically $1000 each participant.

3. It is potentially highly destructive to the vulnerable vegetation which can take years to recover.

4. Your friendly Ranger might put you on a chain gang to smooth out the damage you've done. I'm not kidding.

5. You will be hated.

This applies everywhere, even on beach sand, although driving on a beach does not carry the hatred penalty and may not harm the environment. There is one clean exception: on snow over frozen ground/glacier it's okay, environmentally, legally and hatred-ly.

Moss:

Iceland has many lava fields, often only thousands or even hundreds of years old. The lava is covered with thick moss, which is softer than your bed and if the underlay is the right shape, good to sleep on or do whatever a vivid imagination permits. Therefore a lava field can easily be

This is either moss, or the slime eruption of death

described as a sofa, only bigger and more difficult to rotate.

Ripping up moss is a **NO-NO.** Seriously.

Reasons:

1. It is completely illegal.   2. It carries a heavy fine.

3. Moss takes something like a thousand years to grow back. Really.

4. You will be hated, vilified and ridiculed.

Carving your name into the landscape is a **NO-NO.**

Reasons: Same reasons you don't want Brad Pitt carving a swastika into your forehead, really. It's illegal and defaces nature.

Adding dye or color to a geyser or any other natural feature is a **NO-NO.**

Reasons: All right, you may consider yourself an artist and therefore above the norms of society. You may be convinced that the chemical you're using breaks down in nature and/or causes no lasting damage. Consider then, that as an artist, as opposed to a scientist, you may not know a whole lot about the behaviour of chemicals and might well be wrong. Also consider that you may be providing inspiration to someone who is an even bigger idiot than you. Just stick to canvas.

DON'T abuse the staff of public institutions.

Reasons:

The Mail logo

1. You are a guest.

2. If things work differently from what you were expecting, there's nobody to blame but yourself.

3. Their wages are paid by us, the locals, so if anybody is going to abuse them, it's us.

Cairns:

This is a big area, plagued by idiots, which requires thorough coverage.

A Cairn (*Varða*) is a pile of rocks, usually taller than it is wide. Its purpose is to guide travellers along overland routes which often are otherwise difficult to track. They usually line traditional routes such that the next one is visible from the present one in questionable weather. Now, if we believe stories written down through the centuries, and we do, then in old Iceland a leading cause of death was walking outside. Even a walk of a few miles from one farm to the next could kill you. How? Simple. You started walking. A storm started. Bada-bing. You would next be seen in the spring. In such a situation, cairns could be the difference between life and death, and that was the whole point. This is a medieval GPS system. You may scoff, but even in this age of apps and satellites a cairn can still save a life. Let's remember that shall we? See chapter 5.

A cairn

Culturally, cairns represent the only public works enacted in Iceland over a thousand-year period. They were started by the Royal Society for Putting Things on Top of Other Things.[27] They are our pyramids. Yes, ha-ha, very funny. Okay, they're ours, and we're proud of them. Well, not proud as such. But at least they're there.

A couple of cairns (left; far right) guarding a path

Destroying a cairn or removing rocks from one is a **NO-NO.** Hatred and vilification, etc.

---

[27] No they weren't

DON'T build new cairns.

Reasons:

1. The GPS satellite system is pretty nifty, but you wouldn't throw junk into space even if you could, would you? The space police would send you up with a litter prod.

2. Iceland is not a make-your-own theme park.

3. It is cultural pollution.

4. It could lead a traveller astray and cause death.

5. You will be ridiculed and despised.

6. You could encourage others - so not even inside a town m'kay.

DO add rocks to existing cairns.

Reasons: This is actually a customary duty of the traveller and is encouraged. So, if you want to have good, traditional fun and earn the respect of locals, knock yourself out. Build it as big as you like but try to preserve the general shape. You could even win *Tourist of the Month*. Do note in this instance that cairns don't exist in tight groups in a small area - those would be false ones, started by idiots. Just keep walking.

DO defer to the locals when out in the wild.

Reasons: Keep in mind that there are nature lovers among the locals too, and until recently they've had this mad country to themselves, enjoying the stillness and solitude to the fullest. Perhaps bumping into one other hiker on a bad day. Now they have to put up with swarms of people in their favorite haunts. It's a situation that could get out of hand. If you notice a local among you, try as best you can not to crowd him. If he has a favorite spot, give it up. You just might prevent tragedy of Hollywood proportions.

DON'T poop.

Reasons: Okay, this is a difficult one. There's a lack of toilets, there, I said it. But even I realise that when you've got to go you've got to go. Small towns are major victims of the Poop Wars. Let's remember that the towns are small, and can easily get pooped out, but the country is large and can take a lot of shit. Just make the effort to get well out of habitation and areas people are likely to frequent and either dig a hole or put it under a rock - don't leave it on the surface. Nature can take care of the rest, and will even thank you for the A+ grade fertilizer. Then there will be no more talk of shitty tourists. Problem areas include *Landmannalaugar, Skaftafell* and *Mývatn*. If you're going to be frequenting such destinations, it would be a good idea to procure a collapsible shovel, and not only for this purpose.

DON'T dispute global warming.

Reasons: Not that Icelanders are unusually hot for this subject, it's just that the climate here has already warmed so much that everybody over the age of thirty knows it's happening. You'll just be ridiculed. A better use of your time would be to go to Egypt and lecture them on the color of sand. It's black btw.

When staying in a hotel, DON'T keep asking for services that are not clearly or apparently on offer. If you are unhappy with your accommodation, take your business elsewhere.

Reasons: If you have to ask, you'll never make *Tourist of the Month*.

DON'T pet and/or feed horses you encounter on your travels, except by express permission of the owner. You'd do well to make a protest if your tour guide seems to be taking liberties, that'd pretty much ensure a podium finish in *Tourist of the Month*. Go to a petting zoo/farm instead.

Reasons:

1. It can ruin the training process of a ride horse.

2. It can lead to gastrointestinal complications.

3. The horse may even have to be put down.

4. Farmer Jón's got a gun.

DO use sunscreen and sunglasses in the months of May & June (at least) in fine weather.

Reasons: Even though Iceland is the last place where you thought sunlight would give you problems, take note of the following: Icelandic air in springtime is dry and free of particle pollution.  This represents an open door to UV radiation, and you can burn badly in a short time without protection if the sun is out. Take special care in the highlands. The *Shire/Egilsstaðir* also is a danger zone (continental climate).

DO drink from mountain streams. Just take some simple precautions: make sure there's no habitation, agriculture or forestry operation upstream, and then you're OK. Iceland has no large animals like bears that like to mess aorund in streams and rivers and pollute them.

Reasons: It's delicious.

DON'T hack away at rock/silica formations at or near popular attractions or unusual features.

Reasons: How old are you?

DON'T believe it when Icelanders claim to believe in elves.

Reasons: Claiming to believe something exists, and actually believing it, are two different things. There are people in this world who actually believe in things such as black magic - to them it's a cold, hard reality. Pretend to put a spell on them, they'll get so scared they'll do anything you ask. THAT'S believing. If someone tells you they believe in elves, steal their phone. When they ask, "Did you take my phone?", tell them elves took it. See if they buy that explanation. Don't steal anybody's phone though.

DO wash thoroughly with soap from head to toe - WITHOUT a swimming costume - BEFORE stepping into a swimming pool.

Reasons:

1. It's the rules.

2. Swimming pools are not for making soup.

3. The chlorine content of the pools is low and assumes clean patrons.

4. The showers attendant will get on your case if you don't. They are pitiless hard-asses, with no regard for your

state of undress as they chew you out.[28] Believe me you don't want that. See Appendix A.

5. You may be ashamed of your body, but being thought of as a mudcake by your fellow patrons, who give you dirty looks, may be even more embarrassing than showering naked.

DON'T hitchhike.

Reasons:

1. It creates danger by the roadside through unscheduled stops - including for you.

2. Hitchhiking is equivalent to begging. You should pay your way, not sponge off passers-by.

3. Ride sharing is possible. See Appendix B.

DON'T be put off if the locals are curt with you, including service personnel.

Reasons: It's the Icelandic way of speaking. It's short and informal, and not intentionally rude, although not terribly good manners. Honorifics are very rarely used, apart from *Séra* to priests only. We don't even have a word for "please", can you believe that? If so you'll believe anything. It's true though. This all has something to do with the fact that this is traditionally a highly egalitarian society, with no royalty or nobility. Everyone has sucked equally.

This author has personally witnessed the following, and let me emphasise that truer words than these have never been recorded in a tourist guide: A sidewalk café in Reykjavík City Centre. Summer. Middle of the day. The author is sitting at a table, having a conversation with a lady (yes, it's been known!). A waiter (male, Icelandic) is clearing up. A tourist (male, speaking in english) walks up and

---

[28] My grandfather was one, and his job was to force British soldiers to wash, every day was a new struggle. Now here I am telling you this. Some things never change.

tries to grab the waiter's attention. The waiter's *exact* words in response were these, in a short burst: "Are you talking to me?" The reaction of the tourist made it clear he expected next to be shot with an interesting variety of guns. Equally clear was that the waiter was not on the rag or having a Bad Tourist Day, it's just what came naturally. So.... don't take it personally. We're dicks, that's all.

5. Idiot's Death

All right. This is where I, the author, save the life of you, the reader-tourist. Possibly. It's been building up to this. Reading through the preceding pages, you may have felt the whole thing is a little too tongue-in-entirely-the-wrong-cheek. No more of that. Well just a little more. But this is serious. It's deadly serious, as it involves your potential death by idiocy and the embarrassment that goes with it. Therefore, the advice given in this chapter shall be concrete, honest and heartfelt, ignored at the greatest peril. Some activity warned against may seem ridiculous, and no argument there. Yet it is warned against for good reason, and even the more ridiculous it may seem, the more pointed and proven the reason.

The legal situation here is such that it is quite difficult to argue for compensation from a third party on grounds of poor markings, maintenance etc. The general attitude is: if you get hurt it's your own stupid fault! Further, the Icelandic temperament would rather deal with issues after they happen than before, so you absolutely cannot assume that somebody has given serious thought to your safety in any and all situations. Therefore many situations in Iceland are very unsafe indeed, more than might be expected by those who hail from a cotton culture. Welcome to Switzerland's evil twin!

Road Unsafety

There are many good long stretches of road in Iceland, mostly paved, two-lane, single carriageway. The speed limit on paved highways is 90 km/h, or 56 mph. Most fatal road accidents occur on these roads - but this is not where you, the reader-tourist, are at greatest risk. Those are the bad roads and the terrible roads.

The **bad roads** are perhaps so dangerous because they look innocent. Mainly we are talking about fairly well maintained gravel roads, often potholed, where both drivers have to give way in a head-on meeting. Sounds simple, doesn't it? Well... limit your driving speed on these roads. They have a general speed limit of 80 km/h (50 mph) but that is often way too fast. Set your own speed limit at 60 km/h (38 mph) or less on these roads (but be prepared to give way if an impatient local turns up behind you). Take special care and slow down before tarmac ends and a gravel road begins, for two reasons: your tarmac speed may be excessive for gravel; the gravel patch immediately following tarmac is often rougher than usual. When you see a car approaching from head on, slow well down and give way. Be sure to take your foot off the accelerator, this gives you better control and prevents flying pebbles. The problems really start when you DON'T see the car approaching from the other direction. Blind hills are usually marked as such on main route gravel roads - blind turns, not so much. When you see such a marking, go through slowly on

Sharp turn. **Slow down**.

Several turns. **Slow down**.

Blind hill. **Slow down and give way**.

Accident prone area. **Slow down and stay alert**.

Tarmac ends. **Slow down**.

your half of the road only. But then one can never be quite sure. You can NOT assume that the bit of road in front of you that you

97

don't see is laid out sensibly. Whenever you are not completely sure you have a good view of the road ahead, assume a car is coming from the other direction or there's a mad twist in the road. Slow down and give way. Then there are instances such as a blind hill immediately preceding a sharp turn. That can bring you close to nature really fast. Be alert, mind all markings and slow down. Have a codriver call out all road-signs along the way. The most important road signs to watch out for are displayed here, but there are many more, obviously.

Good road. Listen, I didn't say "great"

Now we get on to the **terrible roads**. How do you know if you are on a terrible road or just a bad road? Ok, if the road feels terrible, if you have to think about every single rock that comes into view, that is your best hint. But it might not always be so easy. The road may feel okay, but suddenly you're over a hill, and there is a steep downward slope and along that a sheer 100 meter drop with no markings, warnings or barriers. Just think what that might do to your underwear if the road happens to be icy. Such an example of a terrible road can be found within 20 km of Reykjavík.

Bad road, complete with potholes

Terrible road. They do get terriblerer.

Lethal stuff. So how to guard against this? The danger signs are:

1. It doesn't look or feel like a well travelled route.

2. The route appears to be leaving the inhabited zone.

3. You are in the Westfjords.

So far so good, but what to do if against all expectations you find yourself on a terrible road? The good thing is that meeting another car head-on is much less likely, but the bad thing is that the danger of rolling off in olympic style is much greater. The answer is: Go even slower, 40 km/h (25 mph) or less suggested. If you ever don't have a good view of the road ahead, possible (unmarked?) blind hill, then slow down to a crawl. Really. One lump of tread at a time. If there appears to be a danger of approaching a cliff, deep ravine or such, DON'T wear a seatbelt and when appropriate keep one hand on the door handle. No jokes. Do remember however, that without a seatbelt a crash of the less dramatic sort is far more dangerous, so drive very slowly. When you feel confident to increase speed, remember to put the seatbelt back on.

Sometimes, but not nearly always, a blind hill is secured with a split lane, like this. Go through slow nevertheless - and on the right!

Beware **single-track bridges**. When a vehicle is crossing, traffic in the other direction must wait, so when you approach one, don't just charge ahead. Most of those bridges are short, so you see everything that approaches. A few are long though, so enter slowly and carefully. And for fudge's sake, if you do see a car approaching from the other side, don't make a race of it. The same thing applies at **single-track tunnels**. There, you usually have traffic lights to guide you.

Fords. (That's not the preferred make of car, btw) Treat with utmost caution. Don't try to ford a river except in an all-wheel drive car of the chunky variety if the water seems at all deep. Rivers can swell in a matter of hours such as on a sunny day (meltwaters). If you have to go back the same way you could be forced to wait until morning.

Mind the **sheep** by the roadside, especially if they are spotted on both sides of the road. Slow down. We keep asking why the chicken crossed the road, but there's no mystery as to why the lamb did. If a lamb is spooked it bolts straight for its mother, even if she is across the road. Honk your horn the same way as you vote, early and often; let them know you're coming. That should pre-spook any twitchy lamb that hasn't been to driving school. Driving into a sheep can spin you off the road. Also, you are legally obligated to report any killing of sheep to the local farmer, pay compensation, look at your

Single track bridge. **Slow down and watch for oncoming traffic**.

Single track tunnel. **Slow down, watch for oncoming traffic and traffic lights**.

Ford/unbridged river. **Think hard**.

Roundabout. **Slow down**.

100

shoes and feel the hatred. Otherwise, expect *Wanted* posters for a sheep murderer of questionable ancestry to pop up everywhere.

Roundabouts are common in Iceland, inside built up areas and sometimes even on main highways. They give tourists some grief. The laws on driving into, inside and out of one are nonstandard. Most roundabouts are two-lane, inside lane and outside lane. The lanes are concentric and do not spiral. First of all, take care that you don't just charge into one like a bull, across the raised centre and end up on the other side without an undercarriage. Taking that as read, the rules are as follows:

1. Traffic moves counterclockwise in a roundabout.

2. When entering, traffic in both lanes inside the roundabout has right of way over you.

3. When entering from the left hand lane of the road, you drive into the inside lane of the roundabout, minding traffic in both inside and outside lanes as you enter.

4. When entering from the right hand lane of the road, you drive into the outside lane of the roundabout, minding traffic in the outside lane as you enter.

5. While driving in a roundabout you cannot change lanes. Signal to the left constantly unless you are going to take the next exit, then start signalling to the right. You have right of way over traffic entering.

6. While driving in the outside lane, **traffic leaving from the inside lane has right of way over you!** Maintain a very good idea of what's happening in the inside lane while passing an exit in the outside lane. Stop to give way unless the car on the inside of you is signalling to the left.

7. When exiting from the outside lane, take the right hand lane of the exit road while signalling to the right.

8. When exiting from the inside lane, take the left hand lane of the exit road while signalling to the right. Remember you have right of way over the outside lane when exiting.

Driving on ice is tricky if you've never done it before (duh). One good fortune is that black ice is rare in Iceland. If ice is expected and you're a novice, ask for manual transmission and make sure your rental has studded tires. In idiotspeak, that's metal spikes sticking out of the tread. Drive more slowly than you otherwise would, especially going into turns. If you are unsure of conditions, slow down and feather the brake pedal. Only do this in a safe location where you can be sure there's NO car behind you or approaching from the opposite direction, and going off the road would not result in death. The car's reaction should give you a feel for the available grip. Accelerate slowly and slow down gradually, preferably without using the brakes. Avoid sudden braking. Think ahead, so you don't get into a situation where you have to brake suddenly. There are two alternate ways of braking in slippery conditions:

1. Use the handbrake. Uncouple the transmission and pull the handbrake hard in an emergency but don't touch the brake pedal. Why is that good? Because it locks the rear wheels only and therefore no braking force is applied to the front wheels. That serves to stabilize the car and prevent spin. The regular brakes put most of the braking force on the front wheels, making a dangerous spin somewhat likely. An added bonus is that the front wheels remain steerable, therefore this is a good way to slow down in a bend. **Only use in moderate to highly slippery conditions** - and at own risk. See chapter 7. Additional: Most modern cars have anti-lock brakes, which cannot be disabled. This is of questionable value on a gravel road, since efficient braking can depend on the wheels cutting through the loose top layer. The handbrake can be a **last resort** for an emergency stop on a gravel road, since it locks the rear wheels.

2. Gear down (gear 2 or 3, depending on travel speed) and couple the engine into the transmission. Similar effect to 1 but softer. **Only use in moderate to highly slippery conditions** - and at own risk. See chapter 7.

Once again, allow impatient locals to overtake, and take your foot off the accelerator during a head-on pass.

Driving in snow is an art rather than a science. Manual transmission is preferred. It's very important to use the accelerator with restraint - like a benevolent dictator would use the secret police. If the car is stopped by the snow take your foot off immediately, or it will dig in. If the car has got stuck there is no point whatsoever in spinning the wheels; 'tis the cardinal sin of the stuckee. If conditions permit, drive somewhat faster than a crawl. Speed is your friend, if you are trying to avoid getting stuck. It will carry you through the thick bits. Also, while the car is still moving it is quite all right to spin the wheels a bit. For this purpose in can be a good idea to disable the traction control. Mind the fuel gauge - a snow-driving car is a thirsty car. Keep a shovel in the boot, even a small, collapsible one can save the day. If you do get stuck and the weather is OK, start digging. Clear ruts in front of all wheels and clear away snow that may be supporting the belly of the car. Hint: if you've brought an honest-to-god long-shafted shovel, get in front of the car and whisk the loose snow to one side in a motion like you were cutting grass with a scythe (you do that all the time, don't you?). This method (invented by the author) is incredibly efficient and saves your strength, also it's a pretty good excercise and doesn't strain your back. Another trick is to take the floor mats from the car and jam them down in front of the wheels - the actual drive wheels that is. (Remember to collect the mats later or you'll get roasted by the rental people). Yet another trick is to gently rock the car back and forth if there's any grip at all, but this takes skill. If you do get completely stuck in a snowstorm, and are forced to wait it out, remember this very important item: If the wind is driving the snow along (drifts are forming) **you mustn't let the engine run**, no matter how cold it gets. Same applies if you are digging, and somebody is inside the car. Reason: The snow may block the exhaust, forcing the fumes into the cabin, killing the occupants. Really. This can happen in a matter of minutes.

Since you likely take delivery of your rental at *Keflavík*, I will recommend a location where you can get to know your rental and practice driving in adverse conditions (if those conditions exist at the time), especially alternative braking as per above. It is *Patterson Field*, an abandoned airfield immediately south of *Keflavík/Njarðvík*, on the road to *Hafnir*, see map of the southwest in chapter 1. It is lined with nuclear-hardened sheds, easily spotted. This is a very safe area for this purpose, though not quite virtual reality. Take all due precaution.

Never park your car or stop for any duration at the roadside on the highway unless you are able to move your vehicle **completely** off the traffic lane - and one other thing since we are on this subject: DON'T **stand around on the highway** in pitch black darkness in the middle of the night. Just don't.

Visiting the less hospitable corners of Iceland by car requires a certain amount of driving skill, this might have dawned on you already. If by any chance you got your driver's licence (I won't say in a cereal packet) by learning on a simulator, and you have never actually driven an actual car before (this has been known), I have two things to say: 1. Welcome to hell. 2. Only drive on tarmac roads during your stay. This is the author's firm advice.

Another, completely last and final thing on this subject: If you rent a car with satnav, do trust your eyes better than the satnav if the two don't agree. If the road connects with a bridge, but the satnav indicates the route goes into the ravine across some huge boulders, take the bridge!

The Bad Outdoors

Tourists in Iceland enjoy outdoors pursuits in large measure. This is understandable. What we are talking about here is the queen of The Great Outdoors. But it is not just great, or a queen, it's a killer queen. Now more than ever you, the reader-tourist, must appreciate your position as an idiot. I don't say this for idle kicks and insults. My insults are never idle anyway. There is a serious point here. For contrast, let's look at the locals first. They're mostly idiots, there's no argument there. But on this matter, in this position, how to live and die outdoors in Iceland, they are the Einsteins. You, on the other hand, may be a dentist, or a Doctor of Gender Studies or a pillar of your community where you come from; here however, in this situation, it is important for you to accept that you know nothing. Furthermore, if you are an experienced outdoorsman/woman, a subarctic explorer perhaps, a mountaineer who has conquered the north face of the Eiger, you'd best know that you're the biggest idiot of them all, and in the greatest danger of meeting an embarrassing idiot's death. Why? Because you think you know something. But you don't.

The wilderness of death

Now, the basic premise here is not complicated. Being caught out in the wild in adverse weather in Iceland is lethal.[29] Just how lethal it

---

[29]Someone once said that living on the edge in Iceland is going out in just your pants - that's a starting point I guess

is, is the hard part of drumming into people's heads. Take the outdoorsman who has been on his own in many exotic places, including a several day trek across the wilds of Alaska. Respect! Alaska is a tough place, no denying it. But Alaska is not Iceland. And what, pray, may be this big difference, you ask? Roughly, it is that Iceland is an island in the rough end of the Atlantic, where the winds love to gather. They rush over the highlands with absolutely nothing to stop them or slow them down. They are mercilessly relentless, and windspeeds are very high, as a rule of thumb half hurricane speeds. Alaska, like many other places, has lots of tall trees. Trees slow the wind down and create a more favorable local climate. Iceland has no trees to speak of, so the winds have free rein. Further, in Alaska if you are caught by a storm, you can run into the thick woods and wait it out. Not so here. There's nowhere to run. Likewise, building a shelter is impossible, for lack of wood. Building one out of rocks is not feasible. Finding an adequate cave is a slim chance. So, if you are outside in a typical Icelandic storm, your chances of survival are pretty bad, depending on certain factors. However, if you've always wanted to visit LV-426, this is the next best thing.

If you want to go hiking and such in Iceland, take care of the basics. Windproof pants and jacket, good mittens and hat. Warm underclothes. Further survival gear is a plus, but at least cover the basics. Let me emphasize that this applies in all seasons, even high summer. A storm in the Icelandic highlands is no kind of summer you would want to know. Now... before you start out, have a chat with the locals near your starting point and tell them your plans, if possible. Leave them a map with your intended route. Importantly, LISTEN to them. They are the Einsteins of life and death, remember. Most important: If the locals tell you that your outfit is not good enough, or that the weather forecast spells death for you, **you're not going**. It's that simple. Suck it up and go back to your hostel. Try again another day, in better clothes perhaps. If you ignore this advice, it is quite likely that your body will not be discovered for years. This has happened before, many times. If you don't value your own life, then please keep in mind that if you do get yourself lost in a storm, probably hundreds of volunteer emergency responders will risk their lives searching for you.

Now. What if, in spite of everything, you do get lost in a storm way out there in the wilderness? There are two main scenarios, with vastly different survival odds - depending on whether there's snow or not. Which one is better, you think? No, you're wrong. It is much better in terms of survival to be lost in the snow - IF you know what to do, which I shall now tell you.

Snowstorm - navigating in a blizzard is pretty hopeless for a hiker. Don't waste your strength, you'll never make it through anyway. Stop - and dig a hole for yourself in the snow! - a dugout or snowhouse if you will. Sounds simple doesn't it? Well it is. But you'd have to know to do it.[30] Now you do. Snow is an excellent insulator. It will protect you like a cocoon, or a mother's womb, or you can even imagine you're in a Hobbit's hole and mr. Bean has just blown up a tin of white paint. Don't go mad though. Will the structure stay up, will the wind get through the cracks? Here's where the storm actually HELPS protect you, because the driving snow will seal all openings quickly. There is no worry about oxygen, if the snow is fresh, because it contains lots of air. Victims of avalanches, for example, only suffocate from melting/refreezing about the face, which should not be a problem in a dugout. Wait out the storm. Then, you can walk back in reasonably dry clothes and well rested. When you get back you can tell the story of your ingenuity and survival, and everyone will think you are the business.

Rainstorm or insufficient snow - Man, I wouldn't want to be you in this situation. The best advice is to stay put. That way you conserve your strength and don't get as wet as when walking. Also it

---

[30] By all indications, people of old did not know of this simple survival technique. They just died.

makes it more likely that emergency responders find you before you expire. In a storm you will probably walk aimlessly, and then nobody will know where you have gone. Try to find the best shelter you can - but what you do find will probably not be terribly good. As a desperate measure, build a cairn close to where you are sheltering (you have my special permission in this instance) - then make it a big and bizarre one, with a scarf flying as a flag. It's a way to keep your body temperature up and it may catch the eye of rescuers. With the best of luck the emergency crews will find you and bring you back alive in their all-terrain vehicles. Then you won't want to tell your story, and anyone in the know will think you are a prat and despise you for going out despite the bad weather forecast and all advice. Still, it's a fate not worse than death, and you can appeal to *Google* to be forgotten.

The Inviting but Cruel Sea

Listen, Iceland is not a Water-world with a wave pool. What we have here in terms of sea is one of the nastiest, most homici-  dal oceans on the planet. Next stop *Antarctica* - or *Svalbard*. There is a particular beach where idiots like to gather and play Russian roulette of the wet variety. I won't tell you where or what it's called, for fear of encouraging the idiot in you. But deaths have occurred, complete with embarrassment and loss of face - if the sea scrapes you along the rocks that is. This is not what you want the folks at home to hear. Also keep in mind that you can get others killed - people often jump into the sea in a vain attempt to save somebody else. Really. Just stay away from it. Look, don't touch.

Avoid Rib Boat tours - the impact with the sea is sometimes hard enough to break your back.

The Ice Lagoon of Death

This is to be found in the southeast (*Jökulsárlón*), where the meltwater runoff from Europe's largest glacier (*Vatnajökull*) throbs toward the sea. Belive it or not, it has chunks of ice in it, small chunks and really big chunks. It's like a giant's Martini glass. It is a marvel to behold and a very popular stop. But there are always idiots who feel looking isn't enough, and try to jump on the ice floes. Have you always wanted to be an extra on the set of Titanic? This is the way to achieve it, in that you'll be blue right quick without bothering the make-up lady. Listen, in all seriousness, what if you slip and fall in? (After all, ice is slippery) Hint: - the water has ice in it, so it's REALLY cold. Do you feel lucky, punk? Are you confident that you can climb back up onto a wet ice floe in wet clothes? Within a few minutes in water this temperature you will start to go numb and lose

I know what you're thinking. Don't!

consciousness. Then you sink. Then it's over. Admittedly, no idiot has died in this location to best knowledge - yet. Don't be the first. If you feel an irresistible urge to do something tactile, if looking just isn't enough, you can throw rocks at the ice floes. But mind that seals often visit the lagoon. Don't hit them. Oh yeah, and when you park, remember to put your car in gear and/or use the handbrake.

Fatal Attractions

Some natural attractions are more dangerous than others. A waterfall is more dangerous than a puffin, for example. In Iceland, markings and safety precautions are often lackluster. A path may be marked. There may or may  not be a sign telling you that straying off the path is life-threatening. Do use your own judgement, but conservatively. If you stray off the path, onto that wet grass, next to the canyon below the waterfall, are you really doing something sensible? Connect the dots. Preferably stay on the path at all times. This applies in particular at major waterfalls (Gullfoss is a prime example) and at hot springs. If you put your foot down in the wrong place it may go through a crust of silica into boiling water. Then you get a boiled foot. What if your foot then gets stuck? Can you finish that thought? I'd say it'd be well-done. Stay on the path! And not just that... OK, there are geothermal pools in many locations people can bathe in. But that doesn't mean you should jump into any and every pool that looks inviting. Remember you are supposed to check the temperature before you slip into the bath, same applies here, some of these pools are near boiling temperature. You think I'm being needlessly silly now, don't you? If only.

6. Shearing and Fleecing

Did you already guess that in terms of this chapter, you are the sheep? Anyway, in the previous chapter I saved your life. It is now time for me to save your money (if I haven't already in terms of damaged rental cars). Unfortunately, unlike the previous chapter, the chance for 100% success is not there. I would be much surprised though, if you, the reader-tourist and buyer of a handbook, did not save yourself the price of said book several times over by following the... following advice.

If I welcomed you to Iceland on behalf of the locals, that might be overstating the case a little. They want your money, not your love. What's more, you now find yourself in the middle of a gold rush, and you are the gold. (Okay, so there's an oversupply of metaphors here, but bear with me) Everybody is carving out their claim and squeezing as much out of it as they can, and they're squeezing hard! 2 million clueless tourists in a country of 300.000 scheming shysters - that does put the former at something of a disadvantage as far as market dynamics are concerned. The offers being pushed your way sometimes really are incredible, and not in a good way. The only way the merchants get away with it is because, as far as they are concerned, there's a sucker landing in *Keflavík* every minute. You need to think hard, and think ahead, to avoid being the sheep formerly sporting the golden fleece. (Good save!).

Shopping

So how to avoid the fleecing while shopping? The basic premise to keep in mind here is that prices of goods and services primarily offered to tourists have inflated very considerably, I'd say

as a rule of thumb by 100%, while prices aimed at locals are mostly unaffected (inflation has been low for some time). However, Iceland is an expensive country to begin with, so you're going to take a hit whatever you do. The best you can hope for is to steer clear of those overinflated prices. Therefore, the places to be wary of are:

• **Souvenir shops** - It's a no-brainer isn't it? Locals don't buy souvenirs of where they themselves live. That's your ultimate shearing championship, we're talking $50 T-shirts. Guaranteed, *Leo Getz* would have some choice words in this instance. You can go in and look around, and sure, splash out on a piece. But don't lose your wits in that flood of puffins and sweaters! Make sure you come back out in one piece (and with just one piece - or even two, if you want to take a walk on the wild side).

• **Any shop with visible offers primarily in English** - that's a dead giveaway. At the very least, look critically at the prices.

• **Crowded restaurants where you notice no locals** - That's a pretty good indicator that the shears are coming out. However it's not foolproof - there simply are so many tourists! Take stock of the premises. Does it look and feel like a longstanding, day-to-day sort of operation with formica tabletops and uniformed staff? Then you might be OK. Does it seem like a cowboy outfit or is there some overblown theme going on? Then RUN! Remember: Icelanders are simple folk with simple modern tastes. Therefore, any excessively rustic theme is usually aimed at YOUR pocketbook. Also, if you walk right into a menu in English, but a menu in Icelandic is nowhere to be found or much less visible, also run for it and don't look back.

• **Regular shops in heavily tourist-infested areas** - like Reykjavík City Centre. Don't terminate, but treat with extreme prejudice.

• **Icelandic produce labelled solely or mainly in English** - such as local specialty food. Guaranteed ripoff. Seek out the Icelandic-labelled article.

That's all very well, but everyone has to eat, right? What are the alternatives? First of all, if you are into that whole souvenir thing, if looking and photographing just isn't enough, or if you are Kim Kardashian, there's no cheap alternative that I know of. You can check if Google is still your friend. Otherwise, surrender to the Puffin Shops. Don't fear the Shearer! Learn to enjoy being fleeced.

As for food, you can shop in supermarkets, sure, big idea I know, but worth mentioning (and who knows, you might eventually raise my grocery bill by 100%). Yet sometimes you will want to eat in a restaurant. Then you can find all kinds of fancy places or fast food outlets that will be satisfactory, provided they are mostly catering to locals. Plenty of those in Reykjavík. It's perhaps out on the road where you are in greatest danger from hunger (which precedes the fleecing). They lay all kinds of traps for you there; I've seen things you people wouldn't believe. Motorway service stations are a good choice, and they often have decent variety. One trick (dedicated to all you Germans out there) if you really are in survival mode but still want some relaxing time while you eat: You can start at the supermarket, get some bread and cabbage and dry things. Then go get a burger at some local joint. After you've finished that, go back to the car and fill up on the stuff you bought previously. It may not be classy, but you can derive some satisfaction from beating the system. Stick it to the man with the shears! Listen, I don't mean stab him with shears... whatever.

As much as you need to eat, even more than that you need to drink, and here we come to a major unnecessary cost to the tourist – bottled water. What of it? Well, this: **Don't buy bottled water!** The tap water in Iceland is perfectly safe to drink, and even delicious. There are a few rural exceptions, notably Egilsstaðir, where the tap is fed from a first-class fresh water source but the pipes are historically contaminated and make the water taste bad, although still safe to drink (probably). In Reykjavík and the southwest you will want for nothing in terms of delicious and safe tap water. In fact, the water bottles sold in Icelandic shops are filled from the same source as the tap in your hotel room. (This paragraph alone should now save you the purchase price of this book many times over.)

Okay, then for assorted purchases you might need to make, drinking glasses or whatever. Your motto should be: *When in Rome, shop where the Romans shop.* In medium to larger towns (mostly Akureyri, Reykjavík and the southwest) you'll find something resembling a mall, or even a megastore. That's your safe space. In smaller towns, sellers of utilitarian items don't cater much to tourists so there shouldn't be a problem. Always check if they have a lot of signs in English, they are the Danger Signs. Another useful motto could be: *Only enter where you're not invited.*

Accommodation

There's a lot of variety and range and I won't even attempt to cover it properly. At the low end you have hostels and campsites. In the middle there's a bewildering array of small hotels, and in Reykjavík there are also international hotel chains represented. The unifying theme seems to be that accommodation is expensive. In summer most places are fully booked. One possibility is to hire a camper van/RV, although I'm not saying it's cheap, or necessarily a good choice. I will point out though that this way you have the transportation licked AND you can go anywhere at any time and not worry about bookings, leaving you free to chase the sun, which can be important if you want to enjoy a holiday in Iceland AND (assuming the van has cooking facilities) lower your food bill considerably - a major consideration since food in Iceland is seriously expensive. Worth looking into. You can also bring your own van on the ferry, that's not cheap either. However, do mind regulations on where you can park your van overnight. You might get into a crunch there. I'd suggest checking out likely destinations in advance, look at their website and/or email them with enquiries. There's a general shortage of such spaces in many towns. Even out in the wild you can park overnight in designated bays only. Search online for campsites in advance.

Transportation

Renting a car is a popular choice. There seems to be healthy competition among rental agencies, so this form of transport can make a lot of sense. However,  there are very serious pitfalls indeed. First of all, remember offroading is illegal. Second of all, do remember those terrible roads. If you want to drive into the highlands, or into the wild at all (even on roads), a regular car with 2-wheel drive simply will not do. What's more, such cars often come with a map showing which areas are out of bounds for this particular vehicle (ask when you rent - this is something you want to take NO chances on). Study this map carefully, and by all means stay on the correct side of the line. Otherwise you run a very real risk of destroying the car (even if you don't roll it over), invalidating any insurance, and being forced to pay the full purchase price of the car. Many idiots have fallen foul of this before, and none have been happy about it. If you go for a 4x4 vehicle, what can I say? Be darned careful and read your insurance conditions. Iceland has a lot of rocks, and some are bigger than others! Even if you are in the SAS, or have Mad Max pretensions, Iceland is not the Libyan desert. If you damage this kind of car, it's going to be that much more expensive. Be wary of fording. Glacial rivers have rough bottoms. Many expensive vehicles already lie abandoned in Icelandic rivers.

A generally cheaper way to move about than renting, is bussing. The Reykjavík bus system now reaches halfway around the country, or more. Also there is dedicated long-distance bussing. There's nothing particular to look out for here. See Appendix B.

Local flights are expensive at short notice, especially in summer.

However, if you plan ahead and book your flights weeks in advance, you get a much better deal. Note however, that this approach negates a favored tactic, that of chasing the sun.

Ridesharing is available, but obviously not completely reliable. You can expect to pay some 10 krónur per kilometre, but don't quote me on that. See Appendix B.

It's a Trap!

Some shops and supermarkets have been known to stock light beer (2,5%) prominently for customers. This is a blatant attempt to sell this crap to unsuspecting tourists, who think they are buying actual beer. Only special government outlets (*Vínbúð*, see chapter 1, / Appendix B) can legally sell alcohol, including beer. So, don't buy "beer" in regular shops or supermarkets. What's more, if you notice something like that, walk away, patronise a different shop. This isn't Spain, and the rest of us don't want that kind of reputation. Don't reward the shearers.

It is somewhat popular to go on a Northern Lights Hunt with a tour guide. Now, I'm not saying they're cheating you, but just think about this for a minute: You're paying someone to deliver something utterly beyond their control - what's wrong with this picture? The short version: You are not going to see the northern lights while on holiday in Iceland, it's that rare. Iceland holds the world record for clouds, if you want to know. Just get it out of your head. Going on a hunt for them is a waste of precious holiday time, and money. If that's not good enough for you, then OK, fair enough, here's the long version: There is some slight chance. But you don't need a tour guide, or a witch-doctor, to make it happen. What you can do is this: Watch the weather forecast (see Appendix B). If it predicts clear skies overnight in winter, then turn your eyes skyward (but not under a lamp post, m'kay) when the time comes. If they're there, you'll spot them. Then you can take a little trip out of town into real country dark, even by Reykjavík Taxi, you don't need to go very far. Even better, assuming you're staying in a hotel in Reykjavík City Centre, all you have to do is follow the north shore of Reykjavík and go as far west as you can. Out there is a strip of undeveloped land and little artificial lighting, and you can see the whole universe[31] (see map, chapter 1). It's walking distance, or you can take the bus. It turns out you don't need someone to point the northern lights out to you, just a little bit of common sense. If you see Aurorae move in a sort of wave pattern it's tradition to vocalize at them in a matching rhythm.[32]

Some establishments introduce themselves with the English word "Discount". There is no discount on offer, however. This may be caused by local merchants' poor grasp of English, perhaps what they mean to say is "Budget". See below.

Tunnelling is increasingly popular in Iceland, even to Java. The *Vaðlaheiðargöng* tunnel (northland) is not yet operational at the time of writing, but if it is at the time of reading - don't use it unless it's free, or you've got more money than time, or weather conditions are bad. It only saves you 8 minutes of an actually very beautiful road.

If somebody tells you the tap water is unsafe to drink, don't believe it (unless it's a health official). That would be a scam to sell you bottled water.

A particular warning to you is this: (this may apply to travel in any country) Avoid situations where you cede control of your budget. If you allow that to happen, you're asking for it. Example: if you

---

[31] You'll also find an island (*Grótta*) with a lighthouse. It's connected to the mainland by a narrow isthmus, which submerges on high tide. Just mind that you don't get caught by the tide if you go out there, or it could be a long night. You don't have to cross over to the island for the northern lights anyway, and it's not a good idea in the dark.

[32] That is a complete lie, but why not do it anyway?

desire a trip of a particular area in a rented car, don't leave it to the travel agent to hire the car. That's a basic yet high-value activity that doesn't require an expert. You should do that yourself to protect your interests.

The Force is Strong with the Consumer

Legal consumer protection is rather good in Iceland. For example, there is a legal requirement that goods on display for sale must be tagged with the full price. Listing "Not Including VAT" is illegal, for example. What's more, if a merchant has tagged a product on display with a price, he/she is legally obligated to sell it to you at that price, if you offer. Claiming a mistake in marking is no defense, so don't take any guff. Incidentally, advertising discount as per above is illegal, unless the price has actually been lowered. "Our merchandise is always on discount" is not recognized. If you are the kind of tourist who likes to ask for things not on offer (see chapter 4), this is your chance. Demand a discount and watch them squirm, even threaten to call the police. This way you stay in the running for *Tourist of the Month*.

It might be all right to point out that things here are not as bad as some other country I already mentioned - yet. We may be greedy, but we're not - that. Prices are fixed. There's no point in haggling (except maybe rustic, own produce etc.), and you won't be cheated even if you order before asking the price. At least I've never heard of it. But always know the price before ordering. It's better to have your eyes pre-watered.

7. Famous Last Words

Okay. We are near the end now, or at least closer to it than in the previous chapter. Time for a few words from the heart. They are not famous. They are mine, and they are not my last. They're just words, OK!

Dear reader-tourist. While reading these pages you may have got the impression that I hate you. I don't. Really. I might feel better when you're not around, but I don't hate you. The fact is, I love you, but it's tough love. Something tells me that you, the reader-tourist, will forgive me the insults and put-downs. I'm not apologizing though.

My core motivation for writing this short work was threefold:

1. Heartbreak, hearing about people needlessly dying or being seriously injured as my guests in the country that I love. I wanted to cover all the main danger areas in one short, accessible work.

2. Concern, that my way of life is being eroded by the arguably excessive number of tourists arriving. I wanted to do my best to enable tourists to, as I am sure they themselves want, cause the least disruption to nature and locals.

3. Money. Nuff said.

The pieces of important advice contained in these pages are given in good faith; Nevertheless, there are some disclaimers to be made (as always in a world filled with idiots):

Neither the author nor the publishers, whoever they may be, assume any responsibility, legal or otherwise, for any mishap, injury, death, property damage, financial loss, loss of prestige, loss of good standing or any negative impact whatsoever that may occur after reading this book. Before putting to use any advice found in this book, seek confirmation of said advice

from experts. Furthermore, the author or publishers make no guarantee as to the accuracy of any piece of information contained in this book. Always seek independent confirmation before relying on any such information.

Dear reader-tourist, go forth now, and do your best not to tear this weird place a new one. Bless og góða ferð!

P.S. Only veteran tourists can be expected to discover all pitfalls and dangers inherent in Iceland travel. If you encounter any such situation not covered by this book, please tell me about it in detail so it can be included in a future version. That's Karma - and a considerable leap in the race for *Tourist of the Month*!

Email me: hrodbjarturik@gmail.com

Appendix A

Translations/Subtitles for Selected Local Skits

1. Fóstbræður: Zealous Showers Attendant / Baðvörður

(00:00) Attendant: Whoa whoa, where are you going, rushing to the pool?
Patron: Yeah sure.
Attendant: Oh yeah, have you washed?
Patron: Yeah, I'm coming out of the shower.
Attendant: Sure, how about soap, did you use soap?
Patron: No, not really, I had a bath yesterday so....
Attendant: [Laughs] Listen, I'm the showers attendant and it's my job to make sure that little mudcakes like this have a wash.
Patron: Listen, sure.....
Attendant: Oh yes, come this way buddy!
Patron: Listen, excuse me...
Attendant: This way, hey, don't put your feet up on the bench.
Patron: Look, this may be a little too...
Attendant: None of this now.
Attendant: Jæja, I've got a little shitcake here with me, just a little shit-fella, jæja, what's this over here?
Patron: This is the washing instructions.
Attendant: That's right, these are the washing instructions, can you see the man?
Patron: Yes.
Attendant: You see the man, do you see the spots on the man?
Patron: Yeah sure, I see them.
Attendant: Ok, point out the spots and tell me where they are located. POINT OUT THE SPOTS AND TELL ME WHERE THEY ARE LO-CATED!
Patron: There's one on the head.

(01:00) Attendant: Right on.
Patron: There's another one in the armpit.
Attendant: Right, the armpits.
Patron: Then there's, on the toes.

121

Attendant: On the toes, yeah.
Patron: And there's one on the crotch.
Attendant: Excuse me?
Patron: On the crotch.
Attendant: I'm sorry I can't hear you. [Laughs] I'm kidding! All right, what do we do with these spots?
Patron: Wash them.
Attendant: Correct. What with?
Patron: Soap?
Attendant: With soap! That's just what we're gonna do, little shitstain! [Laughs]
Attendant: All right, over here, in the shower! Trunks off!
Patron: Listen...
Attendant: Mudcake!
Patron: I can take care of this myself!
Attendant: Trunks off I said! We're gonna soap this.
Patron: Listen, I can soap... I can take care of this myself. I don't need...
Attendant: Let's soap this up, come on. Armpits.
Patron: This may be going a little too far.
Attendant: And the head. Close them peepers! [Chuckles]
Patron: Yeah OK...
Attendant: Then it's buttville!
Patron: Listen, this is going too far! I can take care of this myself!

(02:00) Attendant: Then it's mr. peepee.
Patron: Listen we're going a bit too far here.
Attendant: Mudcake, doesn't know how to wash.
Attendant: We mustn't forget our toes.
Patron: Yeah sure, we're good.
Attendant: And the other side, the toes over here. Now rinse! Okay, trunks on now! Trunks on, and get in the pool!
Patron: Listen, I need to have...
Attendant: Get in the pool!
Attendant: Jæja, are you mudcakes forgetting anything? Didn't think so.

2. Fóstbræður: The Foot of Death / Fótur dauðans

(00:00) Narrator/caption: The foot of death!

122

Husband: Is this foot odour yours, my dear?
Wife: Nope. I thought it was yours.

(01:00) Narrator/caption: The foot of death!

3. Fóstbræður: What about Grandpa?/Hvað á að gera við afa?

(00:00) Man 1: Jæja, now we are all gathered here, the siblings, with partners, and we all know what the issue is. The problem is, what to do with grandpa.
Woman 1: Yeah, poor fella, he just keeps getting crazier since grandma died. We have a bit of a problem. There are only two ways to deal with this. Either one of us is going to keep him, or we put him in a home.
Man 2: Well, for me it's out of the question to put grandpa in some nursing home.
Woman 1: Can you take him in?
Man 2: No, my flat is way too small.
Man 1: Stefán, your dwelling is a large one.
Man 3: Yup, it's just that I'm away so much. There's nobody there to take care of him. Also, there's my trip to Norway in May and I'll be there all summer.

(01:00) Man 1: But Gunna, what about you two?
Woman 1: No, we're afraid to, because of the children.
Man 4: The old man is getting too crazy. It wouldn't work.
Woman 2: Us, we're not prepared to. Especially since Davíð got ill.
Woman 1: Then I don't see any other way but to put him in a home.
Man 2: Yeah, I don't like it.
Man 1: It seems to be the only possible way.
Man 2: I might have an idea that could work for us. How about if we take him out to the sticks somewhere, and shoot him?

(02:00) Grandpa: Let's have a look at nature.
Man 2: Walk around. Yeah, that's always fun.
Grandpa: Sure, the weather is so fine.
Man 2: Jæja, let's stop here, you can look at the rocks.
Grandpa: Yeah, look at the rocks, I'll do that.

(03:00) Man 2: How about if we just put him in a home?

123

4. Limbó: Þorra-food tray / Þorrabakki

(00:00) Patron: Goodday! Do you have any Þorra-food?
Clerk: Sure, would you like a tray?
Patron: I guess so.
Clerk: We have several.
Patron: What is most popular, what can you recommend?
Clerk: I have here (describes traditional Þorra-food ingredients, including pickled rams' testicles).
Patron: Have you got one without pickled rams' testicles?
Clerk: Without pickled rams' testicles?
Patron: Please.
Clerk: This one has (describes the ingredients)
Patron: This one has pickled rams' testicles.
Clerk: Yeah, just a little.
Patron: I don't want that.
Clerk: Here is one with (describes the ingredients but pronounces pickled rams' testicles very fast, "súrsuðum hrútspungum" → "surshrsspum")
Patron: Sorry, what did you say?
Clerk: Lundabagga?
Patron: Before that.
Clerk: Surshrsspum?
Patron: I don't want pickled rams' testicles.
Clerk: No, you don't want pickled rams' testicles.
Patron: Nope.
Clerk: Here's one tray that doesn't contain pickled rams' testicles, it has (describes the ingredients)

(01:00) Patron: I'm sorry, what is this over here?
Clerk: That's cheese.
Patron: It looks exactly like pickled rams' testicles.
Clerk: Yeah sure, but it's cheese.
Patron: What kind of cheese?
Clerk: Rams' cheese.
Patron: Rams' cheese?
Clerk: That's right.
Patron: Doesn't cheese come from milk?
Clerk: Sure.

124

Patron: Oh, so you mean, sheep's cheese?
Clerk: Oh no, this is rams' cheese, made from rams' milk.
Patron: Rams' milk?
Clerk: Yup. I also have Þorra-milk.
Patron: Þorra-milk?
Clerk: Soured milk.
Patron: Soured milk? Listen, is anybody else serving here?
Clerk: Just a minute, I have a tray for you without pickled rams' testicles. This one has (describes the ingredients)
Patron: Just a minute, just a minute, this is exactly the same tray as before, only you've covered the pickled rams' testicles with the rye bread.
Clerk: No, I have not.
Patron: Really? What's this?
Clerk: Oh. Did I?
Patron: Yes you did do that. You keep offering me the same tray over and over again, only you list the ingredients in a different order each time.
Clerk: Not true!
Patron: Oh yeah? Show me the other trays!
Clerk: Stay behind the counter!
Patron: I demand you sell me a Þorra-tray without pickled rams' testicles!

(02:00) Clerk: Happy now?
Patron: I can't buy this.
Clerk: Why not?
Patron: You've ruined it.
Clerk: Here's one tray without any pickled rams' testicles. It has Þorra-chicken, french Þorra-fries, Þorra-coleslaw, and cocktail sauce.
Patron: Is the sauce not Þorra?
Clerk: Yes, sorry, that is Þorra.
Patron: This doesn't have any pickled rams' testicles, does it?
Clerk: No, none at all.
Patron: I'll kill you if it has pickled rams' testicles.
Clerk: I swear.
Patron: I'll have this then. Do you have any Þorra-Sprite?

5. Fóstbræður: The Party Pooper / Pétur læknir

(00:00) Guest 1: Listen, then the maid says, the bra is in the cupboard

125

on the left! [all laugh] [doorbell]

Host: I'll get that. Just somebody selling signs.

Guest 1: Traffic signs?

Host: Ohh... listen, dr. Pétur is here.

Guest 1: Did you invite him?

Host: No, of course I didn't invite him.

Guest 2: Who is dr. Pétur?

Guest 1: Sævar's cousin. Probably the most boring person in Iceland.

Host: What am I supposed to do?

Guest 2: Just invite him in.

Host: No, he's gonna ruin everything, he'll see there's a party going...

(01:00) Guest 1: I have an idea. Let's hide, so he doesn't figure out there's a party. Bagsy the curtains!

Host: No, that won't work!

Guest 2: Yeah, let's hide.

Guest 1: I can't stand him hanging around all evening.

Dr. Pétur: Good evening I'm collecting for the paper route.

Host: Hi there.

Dr. Pétur: Hi.

Host: Good to see you.

Dr. Pétur: I wish I could say the same about you. Blinked.

Host: Yeah. What can I do for you?

Dr. Pétur: You can start by letting me in here, unless you have a naked woman around. [laughs] Hey check this out, crisps and champaigne!

Host: Listen, I was kinda just going out.

Dr. Pétur: Really?

Host: Yeah I wanted to catch 11 cinema.

Dr. Pétur: Isn't it enough to catch one cinema?

(02:00) Host: I really have to get going.

Dr. Pétur: Come on man, it's only 9 o'clock.

Host: I've got to buy the ticket and...

Dr. Pétur: What, you've got a girlfriend named Gicket?

Host: Well...

Dr. Pétur: I actually came to check on you.

Host: Check on me? I'm doing fine.

Dr. Pétur: How is your genital warts coming along?

Host: Genital warts?

Dr. Pétur: The cream I gave you to put on your dick, is it working?

Host: Yeah, that worked really well.

Dr. Pétur: So it's completely gone?

Host: It's completely disappeared.

Dr. Pétur: Okay, let me have a look. Come on, let me look at your penis. Come on, I'm going to take a look now!

Host: What's this?

Dr. Pétur: Don't be so shy. Yeah, all right, good. There's one big one left, otherwise it's coming along fine.

Host: I really have to go.

(03:00) Dr. Pétur: What about this other problem from the other day, that you couldn't get an erection and couldn't make it with girls and that?

Host: No that's no problem.

Dr. Pétur: I need to talk to an expert about your sexual fantasies regarding domesticated birds, it's highly abnormal...

Guest 1: **Jæja**.

Dr. Pétur: Hah, doesn't invite his favorite cousin to a party.

[Youtube: "Idiots in Iceland - subtitled skits"]

127

Appendix B   <u>Useful Websites</u>

Government weather service website. Presumably the most accurate and detailed forecasts available for Iceland:

- http://en.vedur.is/weather/forecasts/areas/

To hitch a ride with someone (and meet some locals), try this site. It is expected that you share costs by mutual agreement:

- http://www.samferda.is/en/

The Mail. The kind that goes in an envelope:

- https://www.postur.is/en/

Government Liquor. Your least expensive way to a legit drink:

- http://www.vinbudin.is/english/Heim.aspx

Reykjavík Bus system. Local and long distance routes:

- http://www.straeto.is/

Main long-distance bus terminal:

- https://www.bsi.is/

Police (telephone **112** in emergency):

- http://www.logreglan.is/english/

Icelandic currency:

- http://www.cb.is/infrastructures/banknotes-and-coin/

Roadworks Authority, live road conditions:

- http://www.road.is/

Appendix C   The Test/Pub Quiz

If you haven't read all of chapters 1-6 then turn away from this page immediately!

Read this test to the group (who have already read or listened to the whole thing). Write down the answers, or call them out; the first to call out the correct answer gets the points.

1. Name the four aims of this book as stated in chapter 1.
2. An average family can claim what amount of land area? (Ch1)
3. A tourist was last murdered in which year? (Ch1)
4. Who built Reykjavík Airport? (Ch1)
5. Where did the scientific expedition disappear? (Ch1)
6. What particular branch of Scandinaivism is mentioned? (Ch1)
7. What countrywide festival is mentioned? (Ch1)
8. What island was almost wiped out by a volcano? (Ch1)
9. What is the national holiday? (Ch1)
10. How many santas are there (2 correct answers) (Ch1)
11. Beer was legalized in what year? (Ch1)
12. What is the minimum drinking age? (Ch1)
13. What is the estimated number of firearms? (Ch1)
14. What is 5 times better than sushi? (Ch1)
15. What is the dish from hell? (Ch1)
16. Name the small black berries. (Ch1)
17. What's the Icelandic for Gangster Bird? (Ch1)
18. What gets shot as soon as it arrives in Iceland? (Ch1)
19. A puffin looks like a....? (Ch1)
20. What sucks (blood)? (Ch1)
21. Settlers arrived by what type of ship? (Ch2)
22. The Althing was founded in what year? (Ch2)
23. When was the scheduled end of the world? (Ch2)
24. What was the most lethal weapon in the 13. century? (Ch2)
25. What caused Iceland to revert to Denmark from Norway? (Ch2)
26. What were Icelanders not serious about? (Ch2)
27. What were Icelanders serious about? (Ch2)
28. How did Iceland get some real money? Two answers. (Ch2)
29. Scandinavia shared a common language until ca...? (Ch3)
30. Who was the champion writer and warlord? (Ch3)
31. What is the big theme of the sagas? (Ch3)
32. Name a major poem of the early period (two possible). (Ch3)
33. Name the plant used to pinpoint the origin of a poem. (Ch3)
34. Name the race of the ancient gods. (Ch3)
35. Why did Icelanders give up on writing sagas? (Ch3)

36. Who returned from the grave for his betrothed? (Ch3)
37. Who escapes through the powers of her tail? (Ch3)
38. Icelandic is how much harder than German? (Ch3)
39. Name the letter that looks like a surprised p. (Ch3)
40. The Icelandic word for "Helicopter" literally means....? (Ch3)
41. What does "Robert" mean? (Ch3)
42. What name means well thanked advice? (Ch3)
43. Who is an asshole? (Ch3)
44. A *Grýla* signifies what? (Ch3)
45. Kim Kardashian is a what? (Ch3)
46. Tipping is a form of what? (Ch4)
47. Coins are traditionally tossed into....? (Ch4)
48. Moss takes how long to grow back? (Ch4)
49. What should you do with cairns? (Ch4)
50. Small towns are victims of what? (Ch4)
51. Don't buy what in supermarkets? (Ch6)
52. What must you be naked for? (Ch4)
53. Icelandic doesn't have a word for what? (Ch4)
54. What is the speed limit for paved highways? (Ch5)
55. Who are the biggest idiots of them all? (Ch5)
56. Living on the edge in Iceland is...? (Ch5)
57. What should you do in a storm without snow? (Ch5)
58. What should you do in a storm with snow? (Ch5)
59. What shouldn't you do at the Ice Lagoon? (Ch5)
60. What can you do at the Ice Lagoon, if you must? (Ch5)
61. What is less dangerous than a waterfall? (Ch5)
62. What is the author's attitude toward you? (Ch7)
63. Where is the greatest danger of fleecing? (Ch6)
64. What don't you need a tour guide for? (Ch6)
65. A "Discount" sign was probably meant to say...? (Ch6)

Correct Answers

If you haven't taken the test yet then turn away from this page immediately!

Each correct answer is awarded 10 points. Partial scores are allowed, where applicable.

1. Enlighten, Entertain, Save your Life, Save Iceland from you.
2. One sq.km.   3. 1982   4. British Army   5. Lake Askja
6. Egnerism   7. F. of drunken sex   8. Heimaey   9. June 17
10. 9 or 13   11. 1989   12. 20   13. 90.000   14. Graflax
15. Skate   16. Krækiber / Crowberry   17. Kría   18. Polar bears
19. Alcoholic butler   20. Mý   21. Knörr   22. 930   23. 1000
24. Rocks   25. Black Death   26. Religion   27. Population control
28. War profiteering, Marshall aid 29. 1300   30. Snorri Sturluson
31. Duty of revenge   32. Hávamál or Völuspá   33. Mistletoe
34. Æsir   35. Worsening climate and economy
36. The Deacon of Myrká   37. Búkolla   38. 17 times   39. Thorn
40. Whirler   41. Bright fame   42. Tancred   43. An infant
44. Politics of fear   45. Good piece in a dog's mouth
46. Emotional blackmail   47. Flosagjá/Peningagjá
48. 1000 years   49. Add to them   50. Poop Wars   51. Beer
52. Washing at the pools   53. Please   54. 90 km/h (56 mph)
55. Experienced outdoorspeople   56. Going out in just your pants
57. Stay put   58. Dig in   59. Jump on ice floes
60. Throw rocks at ice floes   61. Puffin   62. Tough love
63. Souvenir shops   64. Northern lights   65. "Budget"

Points honor rank for **written** answers:

- 600+ : Honorary Icelander • 550-599 : *Tourist of the Month*
- 500-549 : Scholar • 400-499 : Socially Responsible
- 300-399 : Accidental Tourist • 200-299 : Embarrassment
- 100-199 : Idiot • 50-99 : Death Wish
- Less than 50 : Go home!

Appendix D   Festivals

Dates and locations may not be reliable. Check and confirm before planning. Only events peculiar to Iceland are covered and selected sporting events. Open your internet for details.

"Stardate": Month - week.

Code: C - Cultural   M - Music   L - Local   S - Sport

Local Festivals:

Stardate	Location	Area	Title	Code
2.3	Seyðisfjörður	Eastland	List í ljósi	C
When:	Friday-Saturday 3rd weekend February			
Description:	Arts festival, celebrates coming of the light			

Stardate	Location	Area	Title	Code
3.3	Akranes	Westland	Írskir vetrardagar	L
When:	Thu-Sun 3rd weekend March			
Description:	Faux Irish heritage/family festival			

Stardate	Location	Area	Title	Code
4.3	Búðardalur, rural	Westland	Jörvagleði	C
When:	Weekend from 3rd Thursday April biannual odd yrs			
Description:	Cultural festival			

Stardate	Location	Area	Title	Code
4.3	Djúpivogur	Eastland	Hammondhátíð	M
When:	Weekend from 3rd Thursday April			
Description:	Music festival, Hammond Organ			

Stardate	Location	Area	Title	Code
4.3	Akureyri and rural	Northland	Safnadagur	C
When:	Thursday after April 18			
Description:	Museum Day, free entry			

Stardate	Location	Area	Title	Code
5.2	Húsavík	Northland	Skjálfandi	C
When:	Week before middle of May			
Description:	Arts festival			

Stardate	Location	Area	Title	Code
5.4	Akureyri	Northland	Vaka Þjóðlistahátíð	C
When:	Wed - last Saturday May			
Description:	Folk song, dance, music, crafts			

Stardate	Location	Area	Title	Code
X	Patreksfjörður	Westfjords	Skjaldborgarhátíð	C
When:	Whitsun weekend			
Description:	Documentary film festival			

Stardate	Location	Area	Title	Code
6.1	Grímsey	Northland	Grímseyjarhátíð	L
When:	1st weekend June			
Description:	Local, traditional activities			

Stardate	Location	Area	Title	Code
6.1	Heimaey	Westmans	Goslokahátíð	L
When:	1st weekend June			
Description:	Local/family, volcanism remembrance			

Stardate	Location	Area	Title	Code
6.3	Akureyri	Northland	Bíladagar	S
When:	Wed - 3rd Saturday June			
Description:	Motoring, races, burnouts, classics			

Stardate	Location	Area	Title	Code
6.3	Kópasker	Northland	Sólstöðuhátíð	L
When:	Weekend around summer solstice			
Description:	Local/family festival			

Stardate	Location	Area	Title	Code
6.3	Garður	Southwest	Sólseturshátíð	L
When:	Week of summer solstice			
Description:	Local/family festival			

Stardate	Location	Area	Title	Code
6.3	Ólafsfjörður	Northland	Blue North	M
When:	3rd weekend June			
Description:	Music festival, blues			

Stardate	Location	Area	Title	Code
6.3	Vopnafjörður	Eastland	Vopnaskak	L
When:	Week ending 4th Sunday June			
Description:	Local/family festival			

Stardate	Location	Area	Title	Code
6.4	Fjarðabyggð, wild	Eastland	Á fætur	S
When:	8 days ending last Saturday June			
Description:	Hiking/climbing events			

Stardate	Location	Area	Title	Code
7.1	Hólmavík	Westfjords	Hamingjudagar	L
When:	Weekend closest to beginning July			
Description:	Local festival for local people/reunion			

Stardate	Location	Area	Title	Code
7.1	Bolungarvík	Westfjords	Markaðshelgin	L
When:	Thursday - 1st Saturday July			
Description:	Market festival			

Stardate	Location	Area	Title	Code
7.1	Reyðarfjörður	Eastland	Bryggjuhátíðin	L
When:	1st Saturday July			
Description:	Local/family type festival			

Stardate	Location	Area	Title	Code
7.1	Reyðarfjörður	Eastland	Hernámshátíð	C
When:	1st Sunday July			
Description:	Military/occupation (1940) theme			

Stardate	Location	Area	Title	Code
7.1	Akranes	Westland	Írskir dagar	L
When:	Wed-Sun ending 1st weekend July			
Description:	Faux Irish heritage/family festival			

Stardate	Location	Area	Title	Code
7.1	Ólafsvík	Westland	Ólafsvíkurvaka	L
When:	1st weekend July biannual odd yrs			
Description:	Local festival for local people/reunion			

Stardate	Location	Area	Title	Code
7.1	Neskaupstaður	Eastland	Eistnaflug	M
When:	1st week July Wed-Sat			
Description:	Rock music festival			

Stardate	Location	Area	Title	Code
7.2	Siglufjörður	Northland	Þjóðlagahátíð	M
When:	Wed-Sun after 1st Monday in July			
Description:	Folk music festival			

Stardate	Location	Area	Title	Code
7.2	Hrísey	Northland	Hríseyjarhátíð	L
When:	2nd weekend July			
Description:	Local/family festival			

Stardate	Location	Area	Title	Code
7.2	Hellissandur/Rif	Westland	Sandara-/Rifsaragleði	L
When:	Middle July, biannual even yrs			
Description:	Local festival for local people/reunion			

Stardate	Location	Area	Title	Code
7.3	Seyðisfjörður	Eastland	LungA	C
When:	Week after 2nd Sunday July			
Description:	Youth arts festival, wide appeal			

Stardate	Location	Area	Title	Code
7.3	Akureyri, wild	Northland	Gönguvika	S
When:	Middle July			
Description:	Hiking week, planned hiking			

Stardate	Location	Area	Title	Code
7.3	Akureyri	Northland	Hjóladagar	S
When:	Thu - 3rd Sunday July			
Description:	Motorbike days, racing, concerts			

Stardate	Location	Area	Title	Code
7.3	Akureyri, rural	Northland	Miðaldadagar	C
When:	3rd weekend July			
Description:	Medieval trading, culture, activities			

Stardate	Location	Area	Title	Code
7.3	Seyðisfjörður	Eastland	Smiðjuhátíð	C
When:	3rd weekend July			
Description:	Crafts festival			

Stardate	Location	Area	Title	Code
7.4	Fáskrúðsfjörður	Eastland	Franskir dagar	C
When:	Wed-Sun before last Monday July			
Description:	French Connection (sailors) historical remembrance			

Stardate	Location	Area	Title	Code
7.4	Siglufjörður	Northland	Síldarævintýri	C
When:	Weekend before last Monday July			
Description:	Festival of salted herring			

135

Stardate	Location	Area	Title	Code
7.4	Húsavík	Northland	Mærudagar	L
When:	Weekend before last Monday July			
Description:	Local/family festival			

Stardate	Location	Area	Title	Code
7.1-8.1	Seyðisfjörður	Eastland	Bláa kirkjan	M
When:	Wednesdays July - early August			
Description:	Musical events, various genres			

Stardate	Location	Area	Title	Code
8.1	Dalvík	Northland	Fiskidagurinn mikli	C
When:	1st weekend August			
Description:	Fish Day, fisheries activities			

Stardate	Location	Area	Title	Code
8.1	Neskaupstaður	Eastland	Neistaflug	L
When:	Thu-Sun before 1st Monday August			
Description:	Local/family type festival			

Stardate	Location	Area	Title	Code
8.2	Hrafnagil	Northland	Handverkshátíðin	C
When:	Thu-Sun after 1st Monday August			
Description:	Crafts festival, countrywide appeal, large attendance			

Stardate	Location	Area	Title	Code
8.2	Þorlákshöfn	Southland	Hafnardagar	L
When:	2nd weekend August			
Description:	Local/family festival			

Stardate	Location	Area	Title	Code
8.3	Raufarhöfn	Eastland	Sléttugangan	S
When:	3rd Saturday August			
Description:	Long distance hike			

Stardate	Location	Area	Title	Code
8.3	Reykjavík	Reykjavík	Menningarnótt	L
When:	Saturday before 4th Monday August			
Description:	Local/family festival - huge			

Stardate	Location	Area	Title	Code
8.3	Ólafsfjörður	Northland	Berjadagar	M
When:	Thursday - 3rd Sunday August			
Description:	Music festival, Chamber music			

Stardate	Location	Area	Title	Code
8.4	Hvalfjörður, rural	Westland	Hvalfjarðardagar	**L**
When:	Last weekend August			
Description:	Local/family festival			

Stardate	Location	Area	Title	Code
8.4	Sandgerði	Southwest	Sandgerðisdagar	**L**
When:	Week before last Monday August			
Description:	Local/family festival			

Stardate	Location	Area	Title	Code
8.4	Akureyri	Northland	Akureyrarvaka	**L**
When:	Last weekend August			
Description:	Local/family festival - large			

Stardate	Location	Area	Title	Code
8.X	Seyðisfjörður	Eastland	Bæjarhátíð	**L**
When:	Some time August			
Description:	Local/family festival			

Stardate	Location	Area	Title	Code
9.1	Reykjanesbær	Southwest	Ljósanótt	**L**
When:	Wed-Sun 1st week September			
Description:	Large local/family festival			

Stardate	Location	Area	Title	Code
10.2	Akureyri	Northland	Dömulegir dekurdagar	**L**
When:	Thu - 2nd Sunday October			
Description:	Events, activities themed for the ladies			

Stardate	Location	Area	Title	Code
10.2	Vík í Mýrdal	Southland	Regnboginn	**C**
When:	2nd weekend October			
Description:	Arts and culture, stage performance etc.			

Stardate	Location	Area	Title	Code
10.X	Raufarhöfn	Northland	Hrútadagur	**L**
When:	Some time October			
Description:	Rams' festival			

Stardate	Location	Area	Title	Code
10.X	Raufarhöfn	Northland	Menningarvika	**C**
When:	Some time October			
Description:	Culture week			

137

Stardate	Location	Area	Title	Code
10.4	Akranes	Westland	Vökudagar	C
When:	Wed-Mon end October			
Description:	Culture festival			

Stardate	Location	Area	Title	Code
11.1	Vopnafjörður	Eastland	Dagar Myrkurs	C
When:	Week ending 1st Sunday November			
Description:	Cultural festival, celebrates coming of the dark			

Countrywide Festivals:

Stardate	Title	When
1.1	Þrettándinn	January 6
Description:	Last day of Christmas, bonfires, fireworks	

Stardate	Title	When
4.3	Sumardagurinn fyrsti	Thursday after April 18
Description:	First day of summer, parades	

Stardate	Title	When
6.1	Sjómannadagurinn	First Sunday June
Description:	Sailors' Day, seaside events	

Stardate	Title	When
6.3	Þjóðhátíðardagurinn	June 17
Description:	National Holiday (1944), parades, events	

Stardate	Title	When
8.1	Verslunarmannahelgin	Weekend - 1st Monday August
Description:	Festival of Drunken Sex, music, tenting	

Stardate	Title	When
12.1	Fullveldisdagurinn	December 1
Description:	Independence Day (1918), low key	